Adult Coloring Books Birds, Butterflies And Flowers

30 Large Format Adult Coloring Books with High Quality Patterns
for Stress Relief and Relaxation

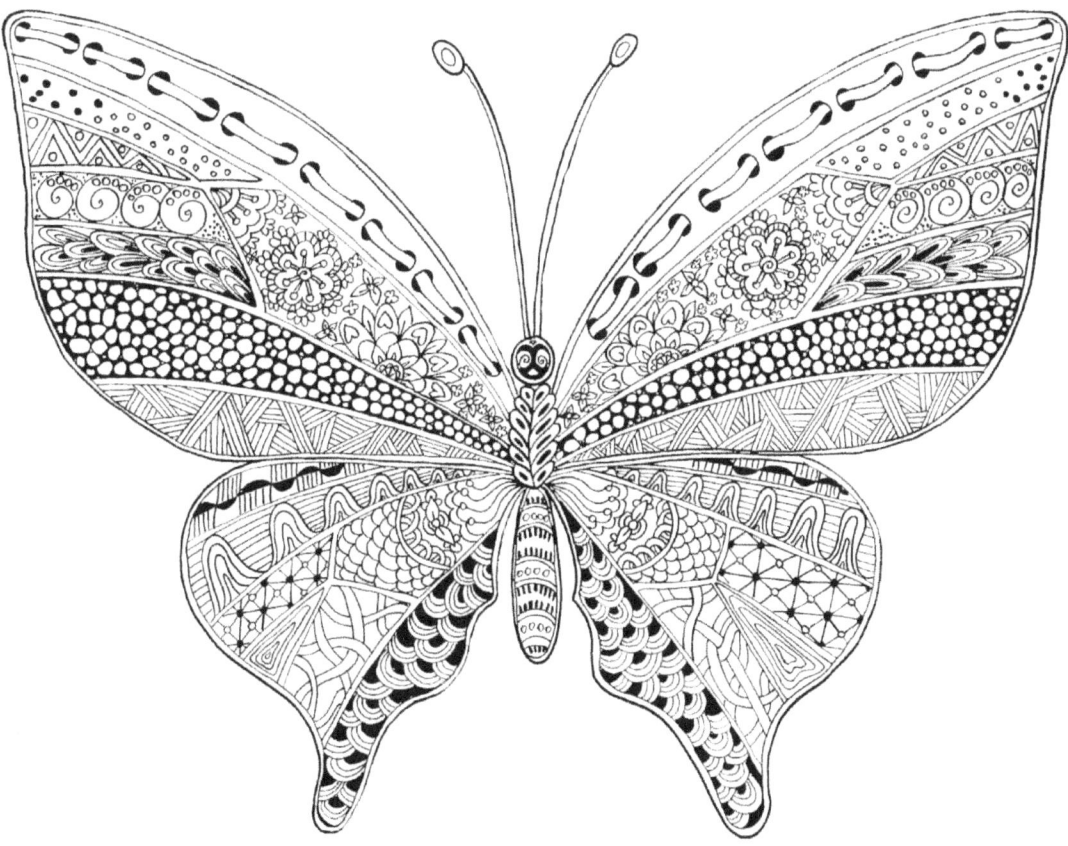

Jennifer DeMoines

Adult Coloring Book
Birds, Butterflies and Flowers

Coloring Book with 30 Large Format Pages of High Quality Patterns for Stress Relief and Relaxation

Kindle Users! To make it easy for you to start coloring right away, we are including a FREE direct download link to a high-resolution downloadable version of this book for printing at home at the end of this book.

If you want to purchase a printed, hard copy of this book, delivered to your home, please see the paperback version link on the Amazon page for this book.

Happy coloring!

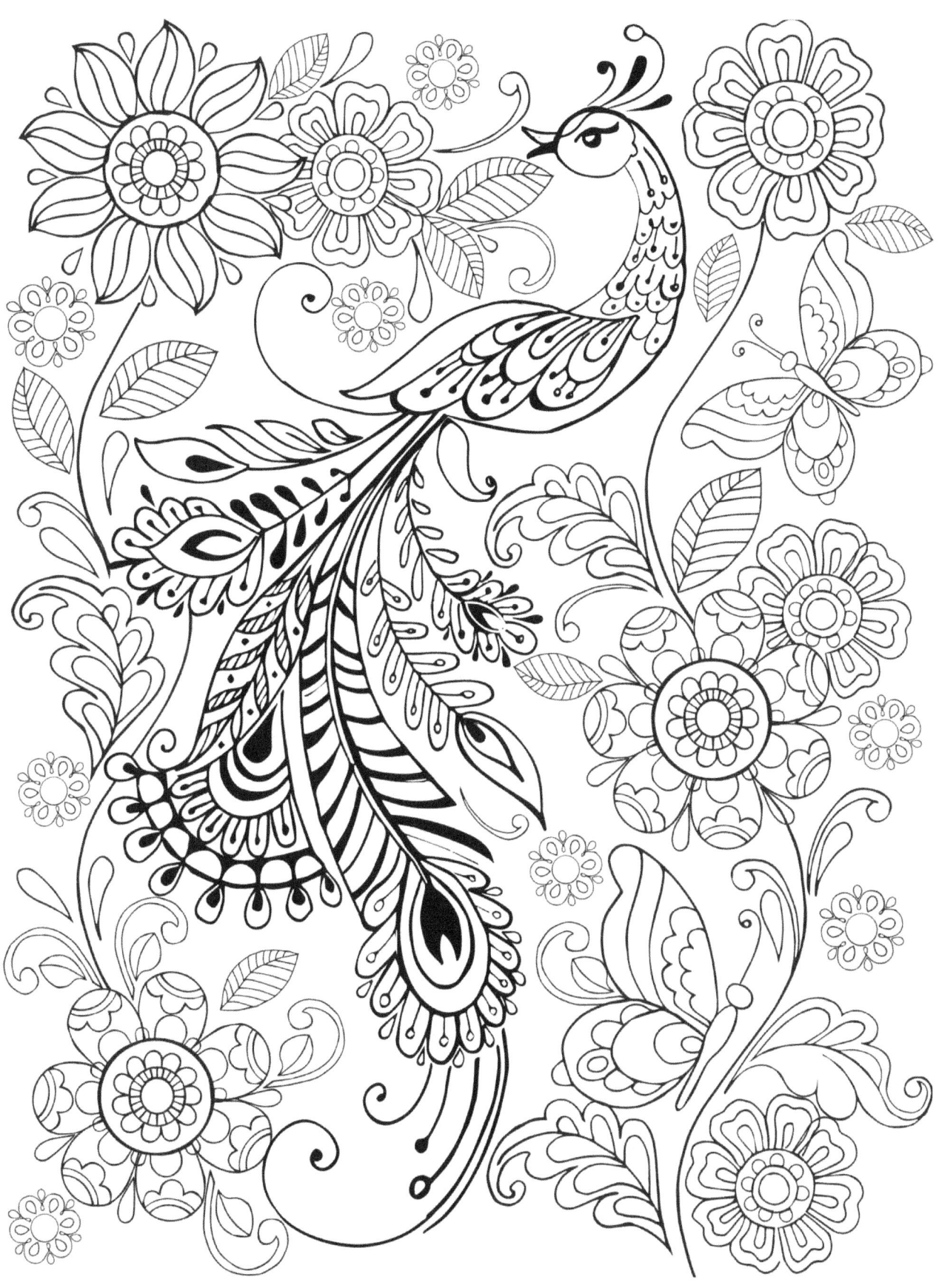

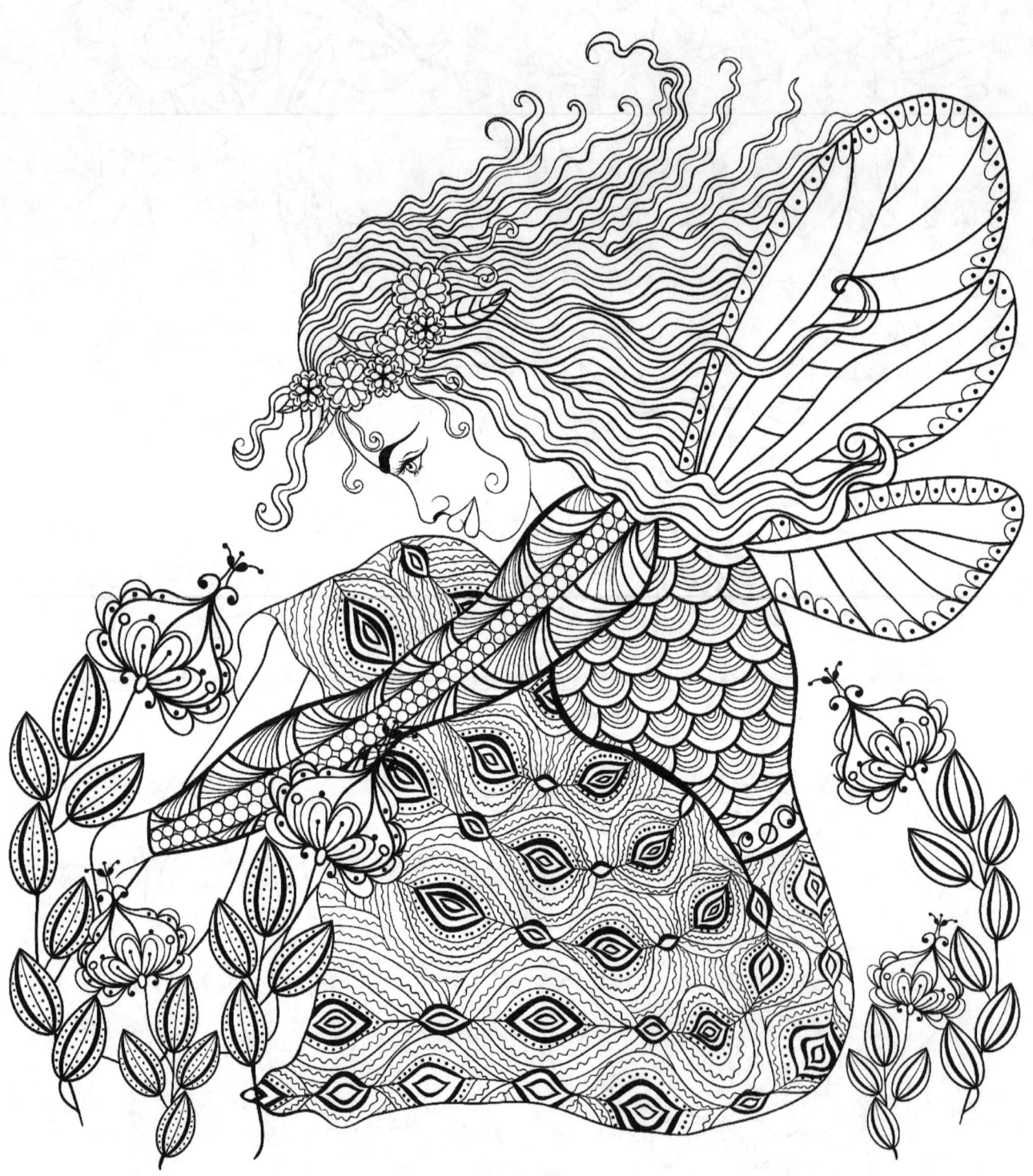

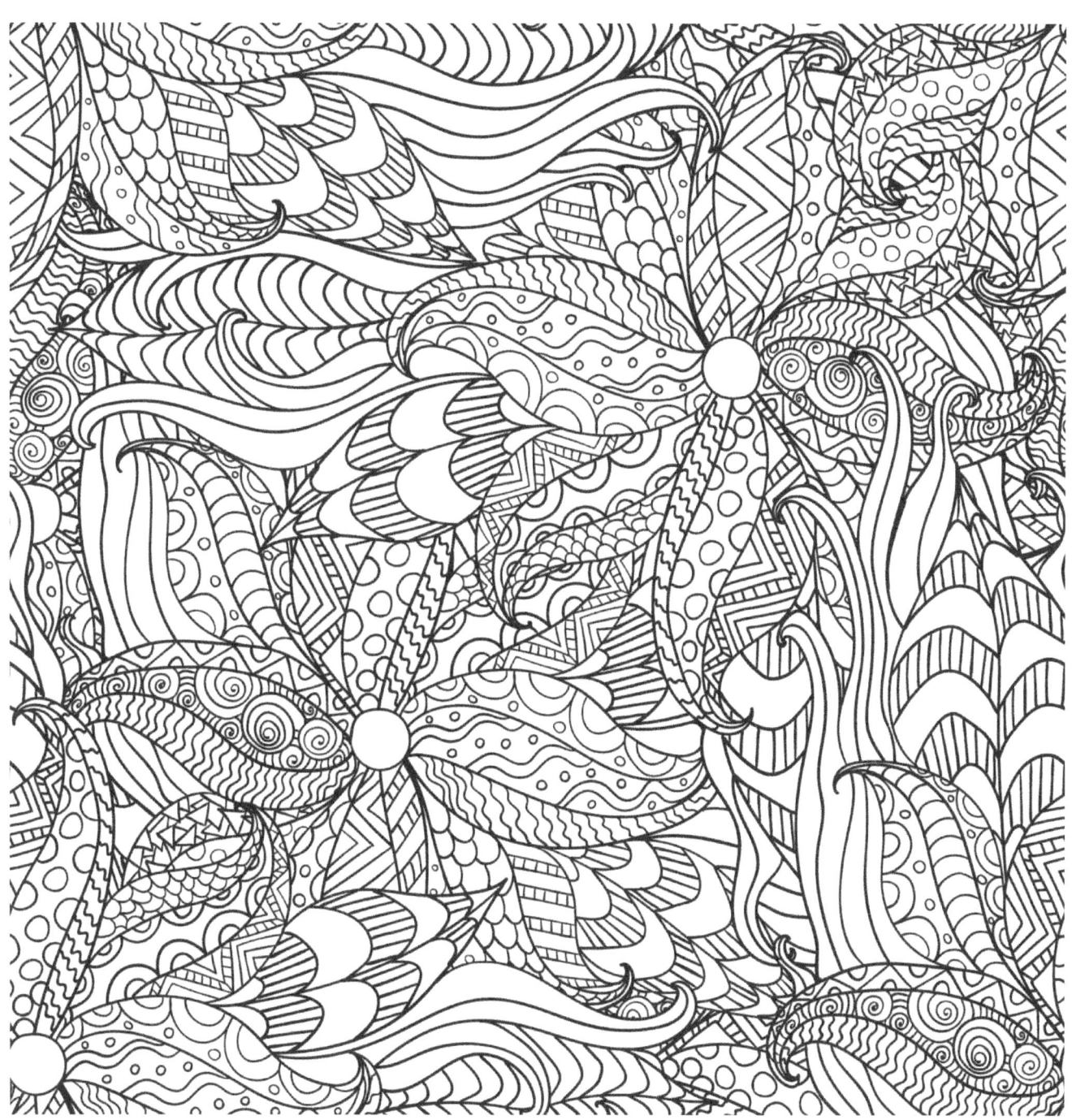

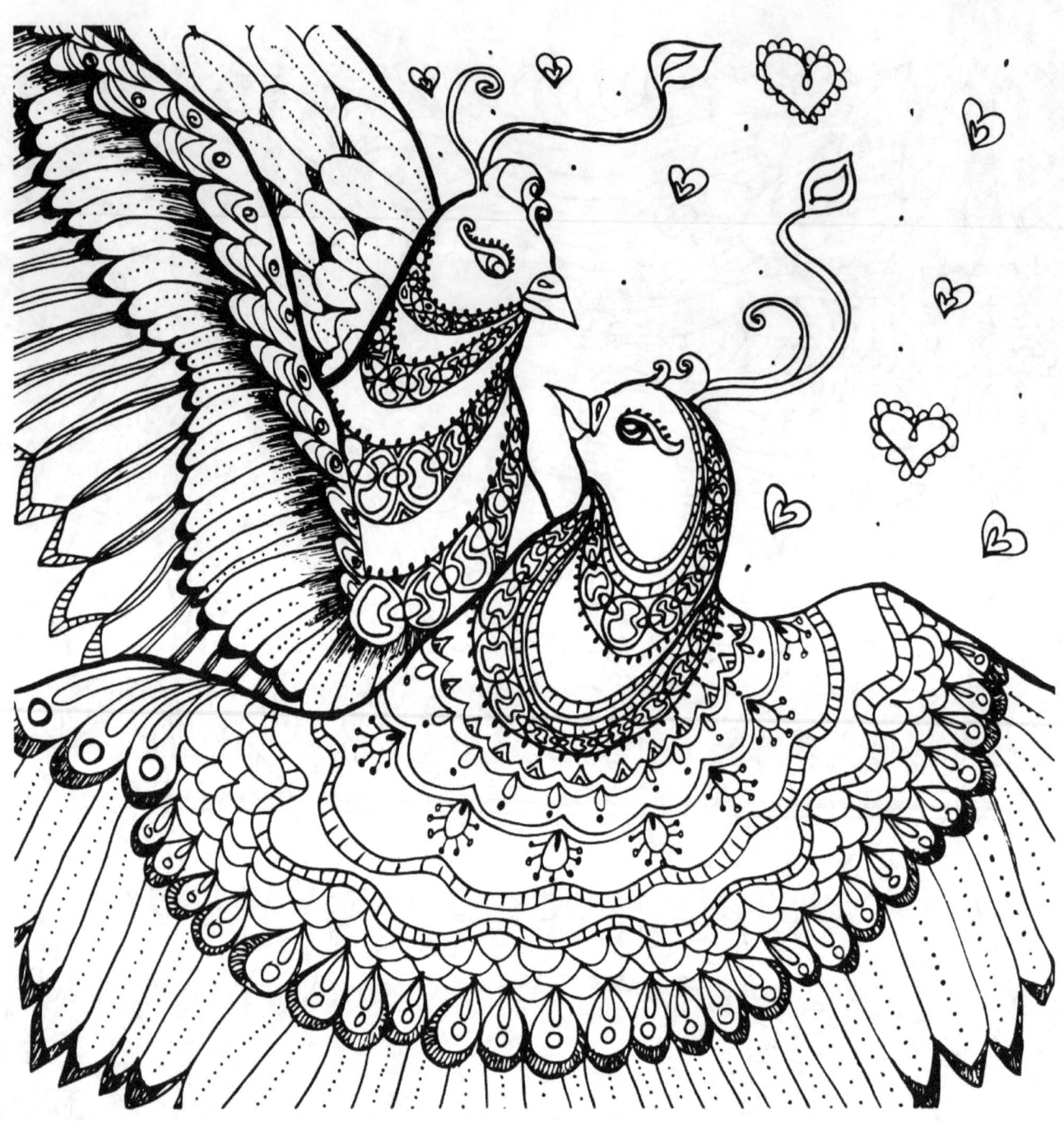

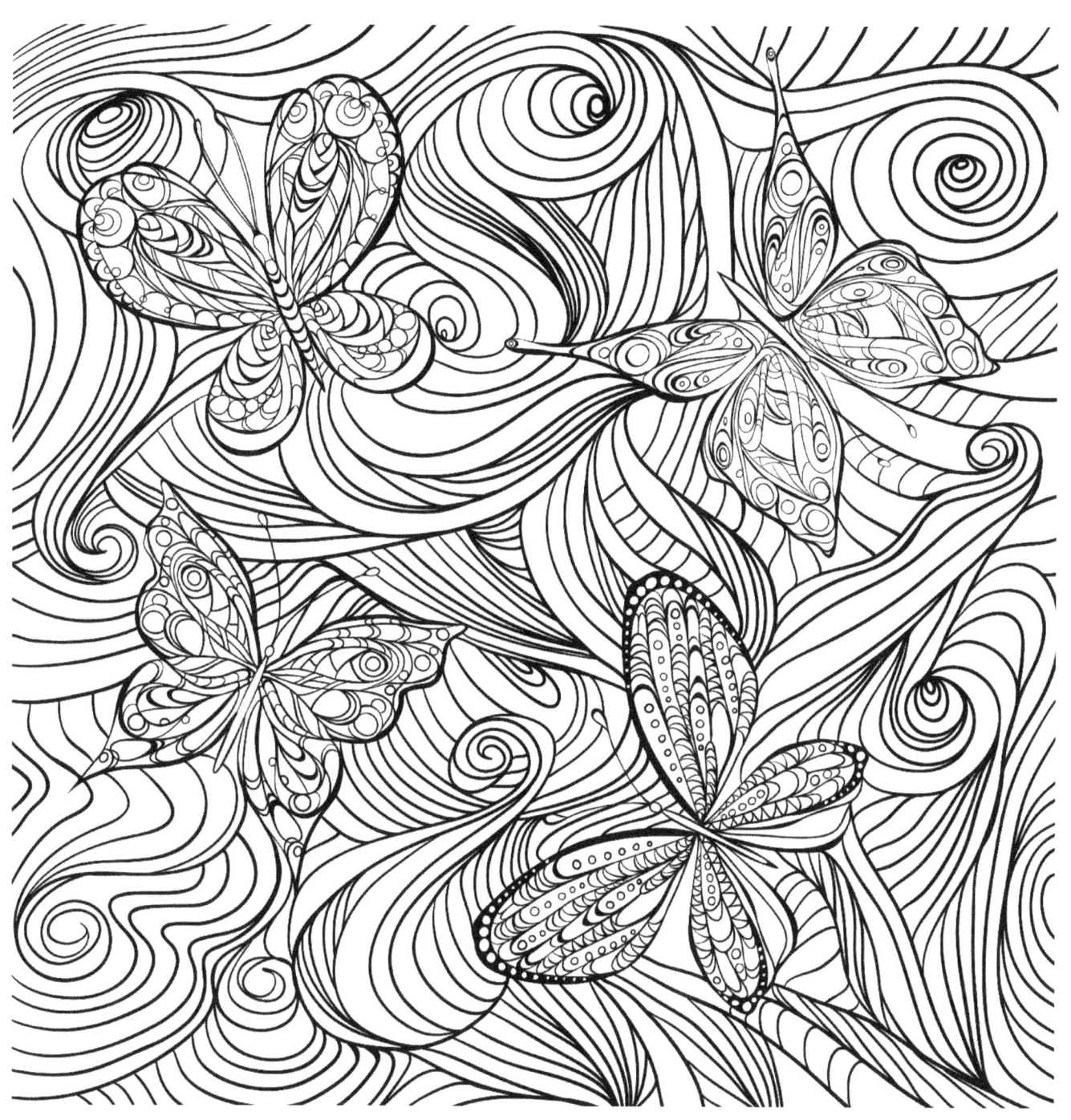

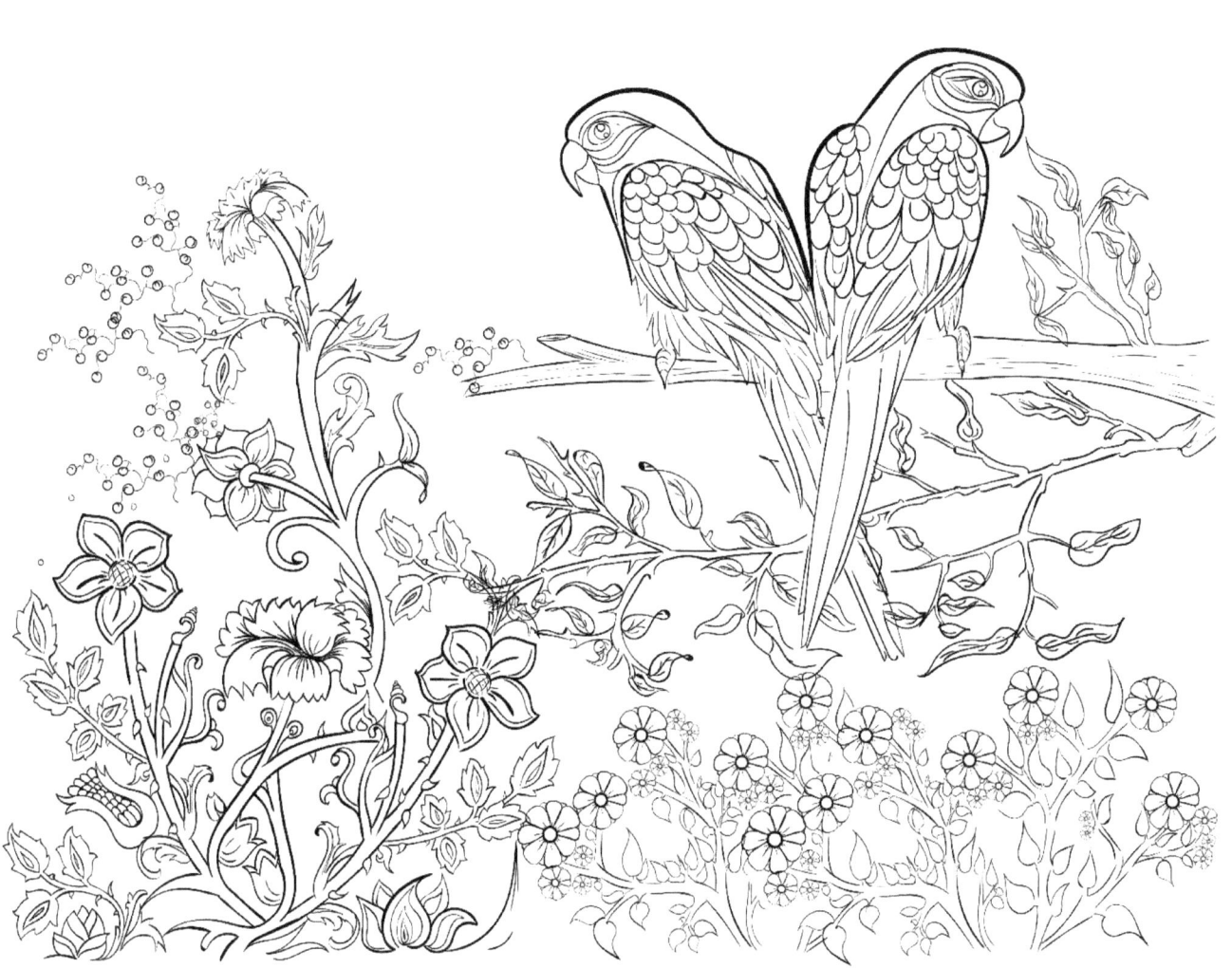

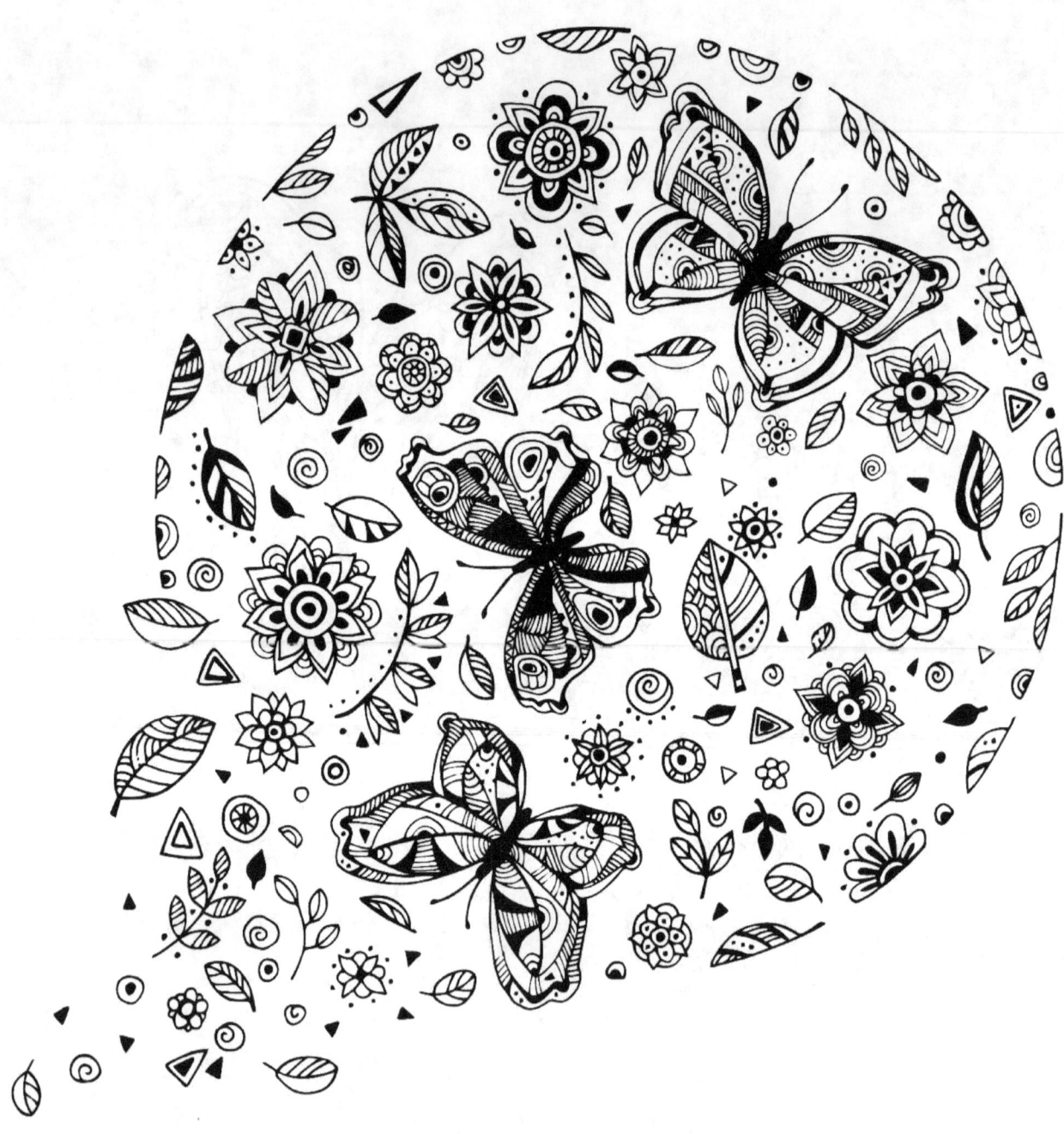

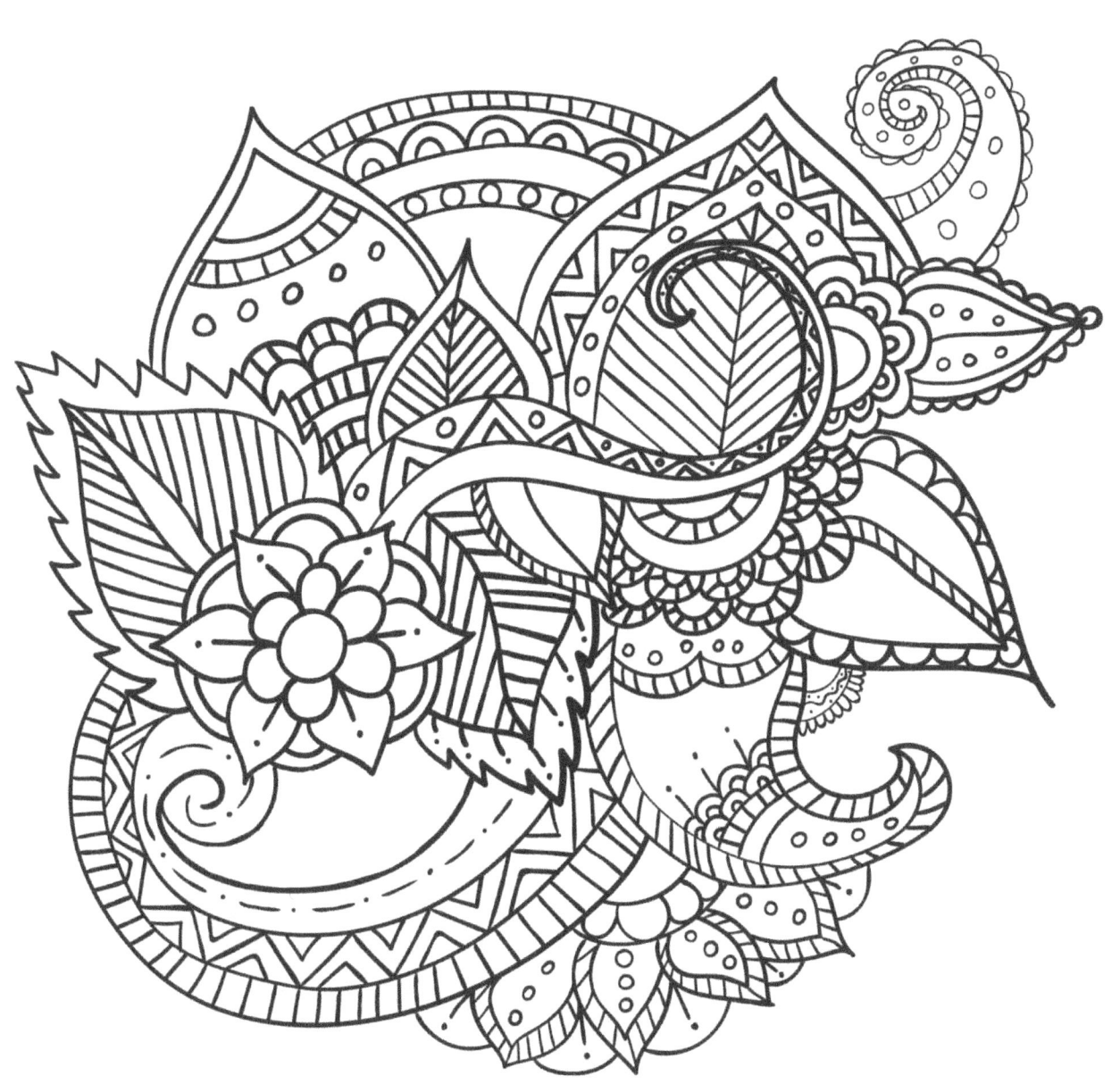

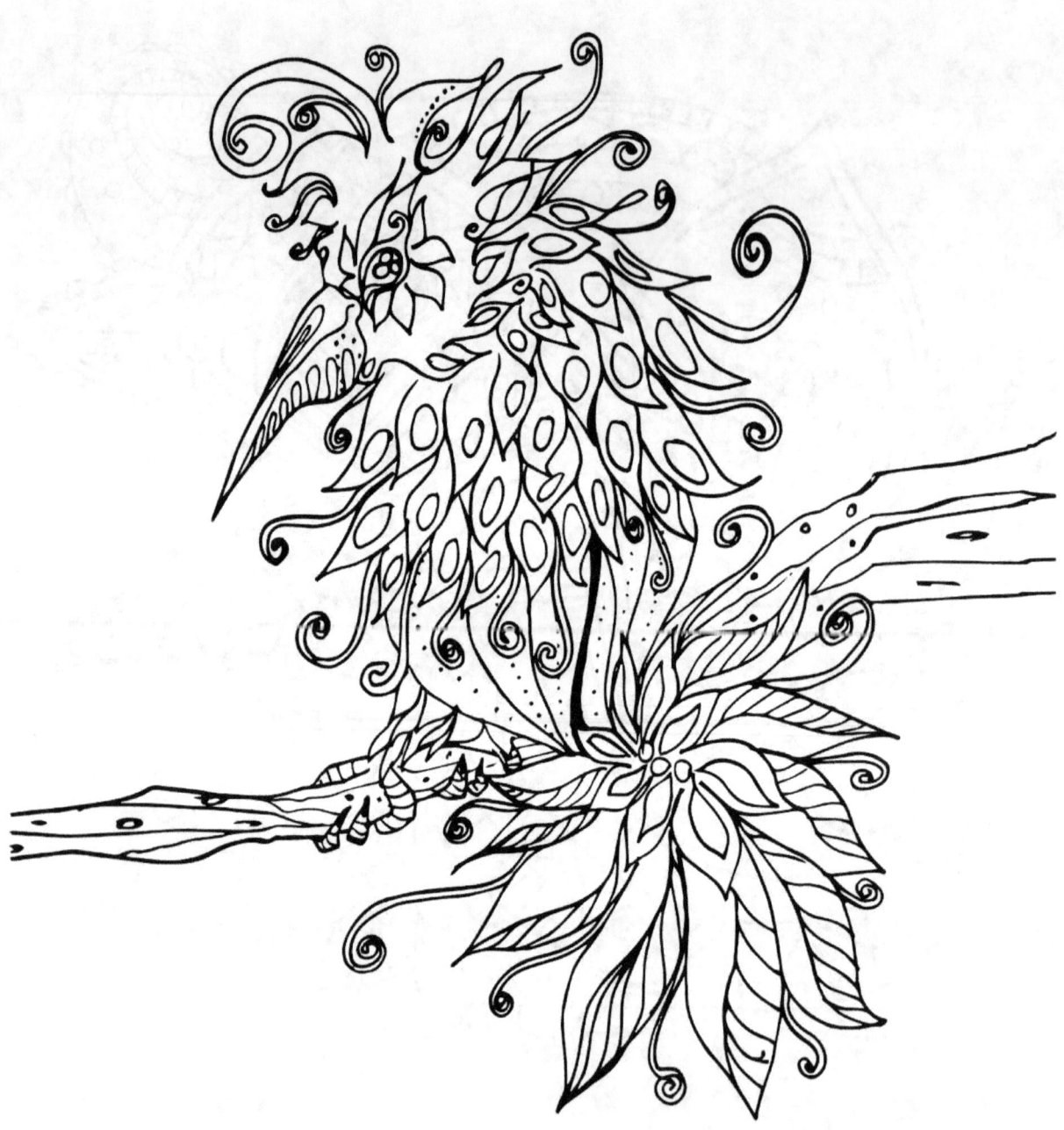

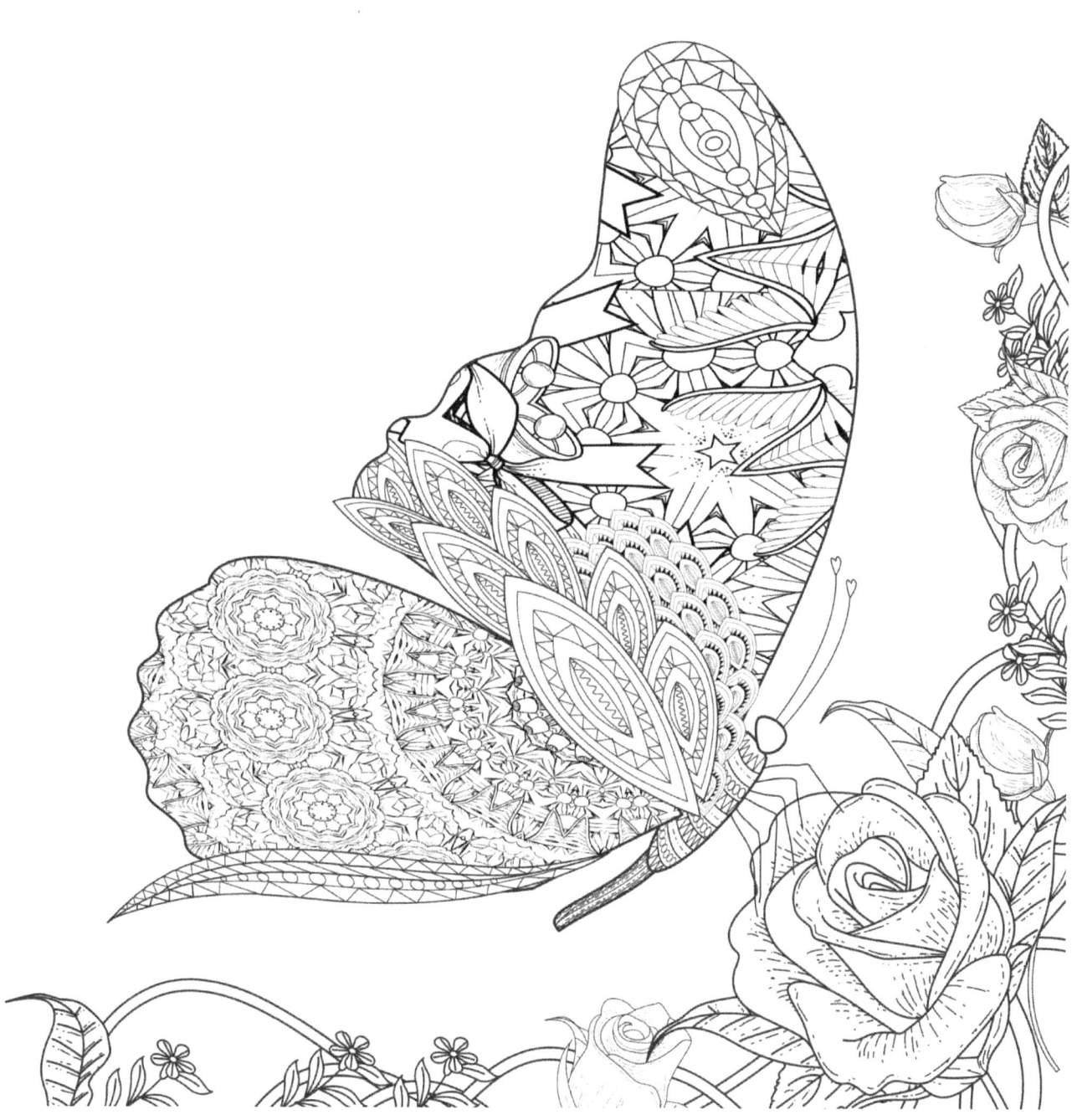

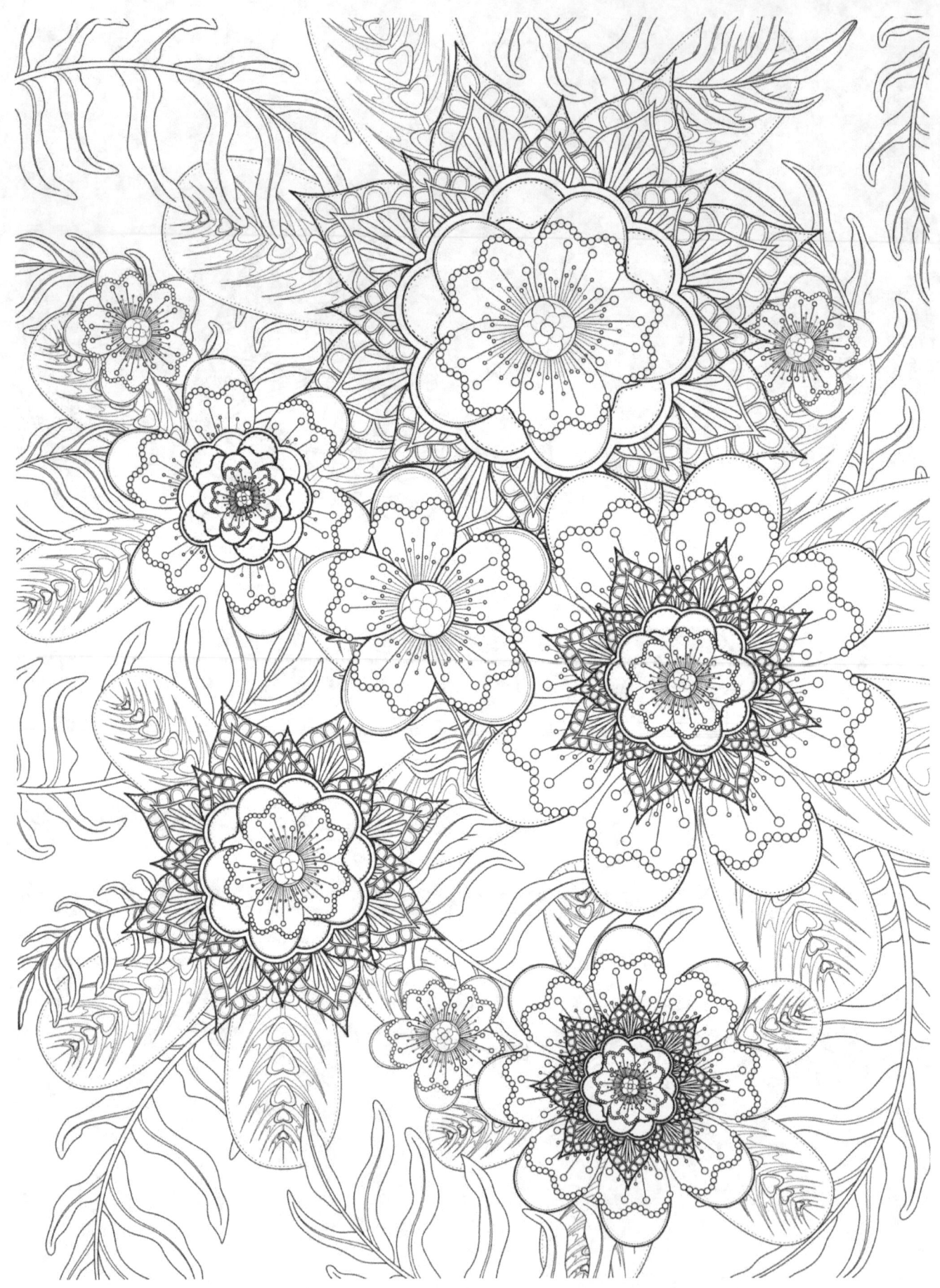

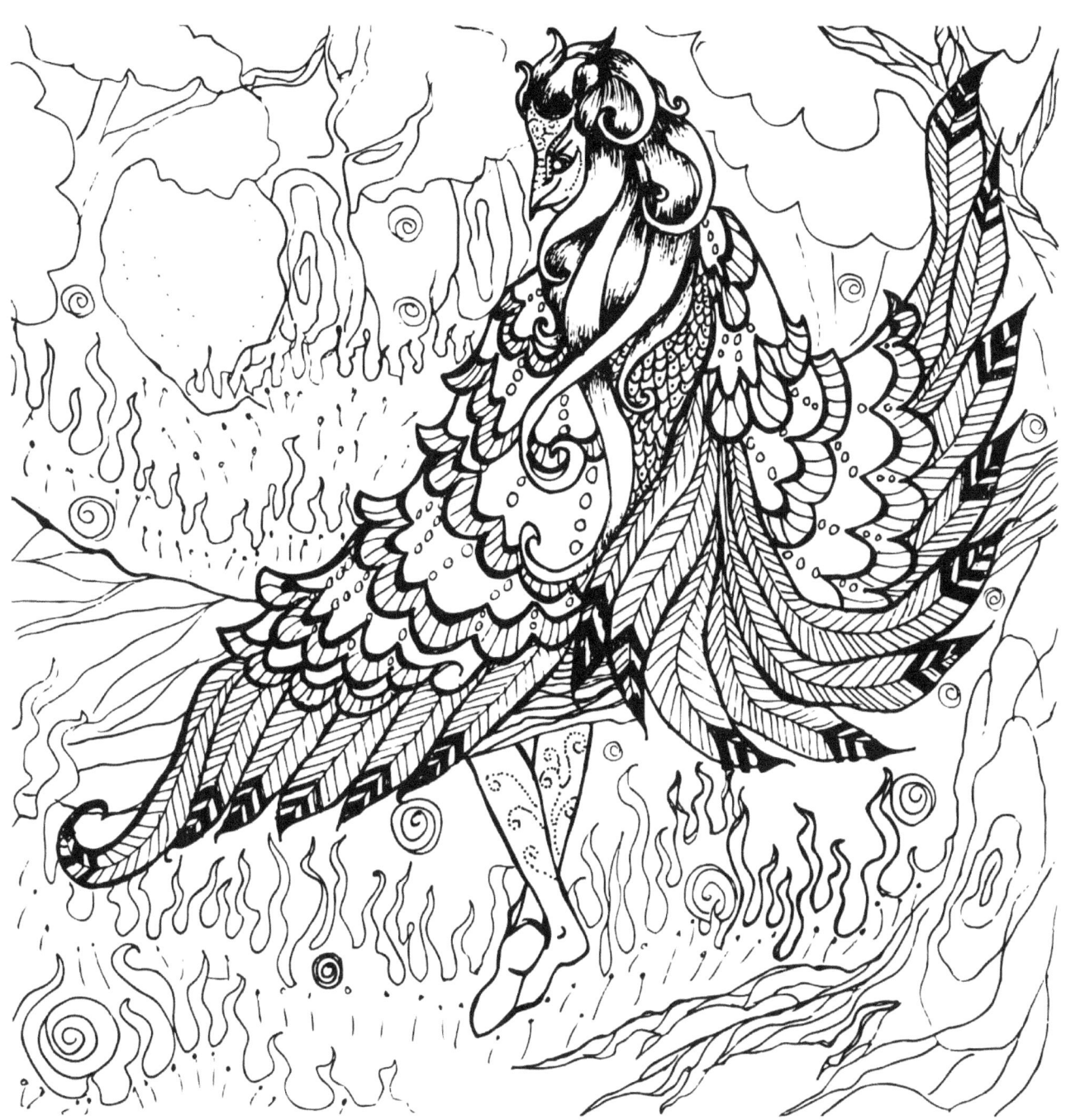

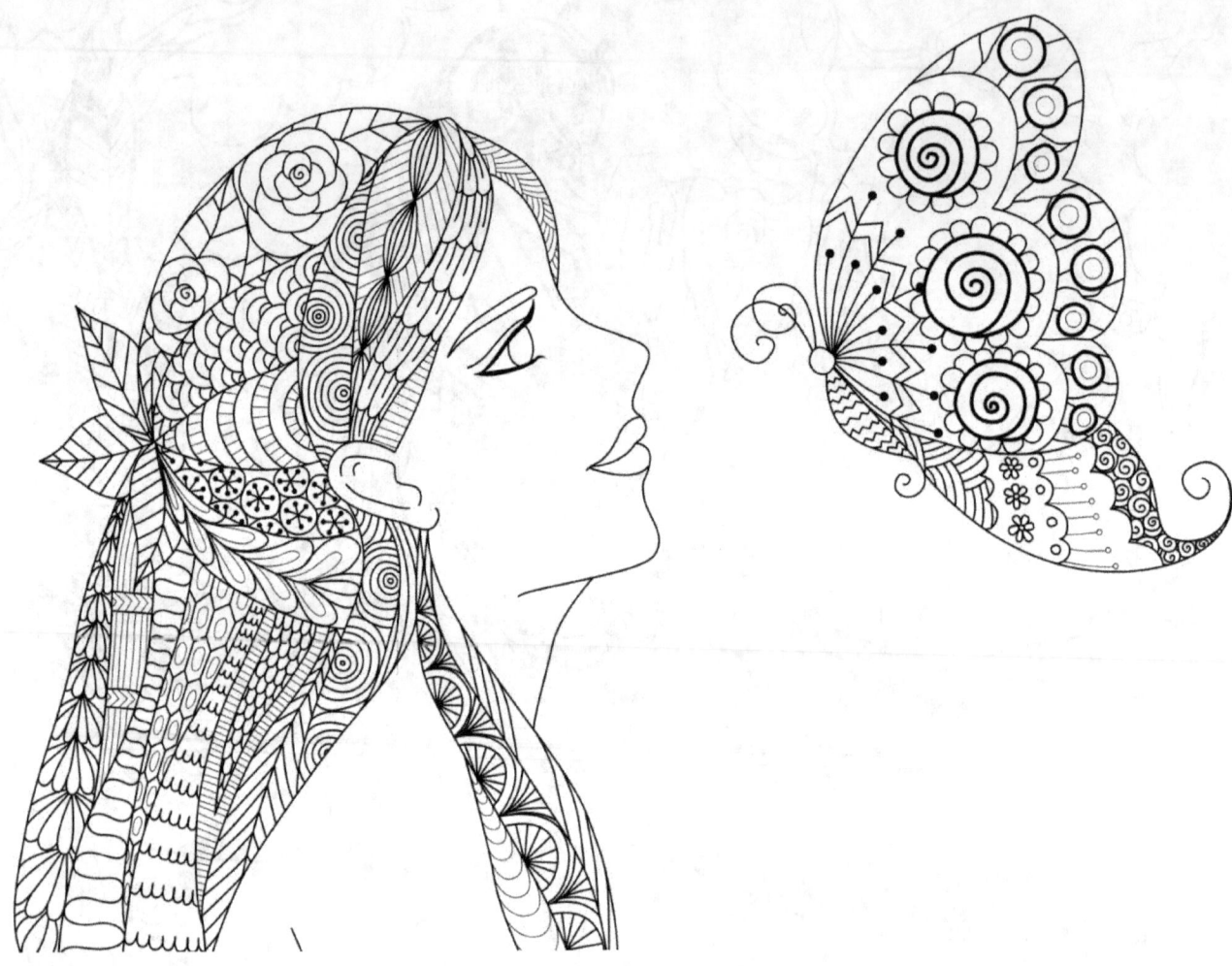

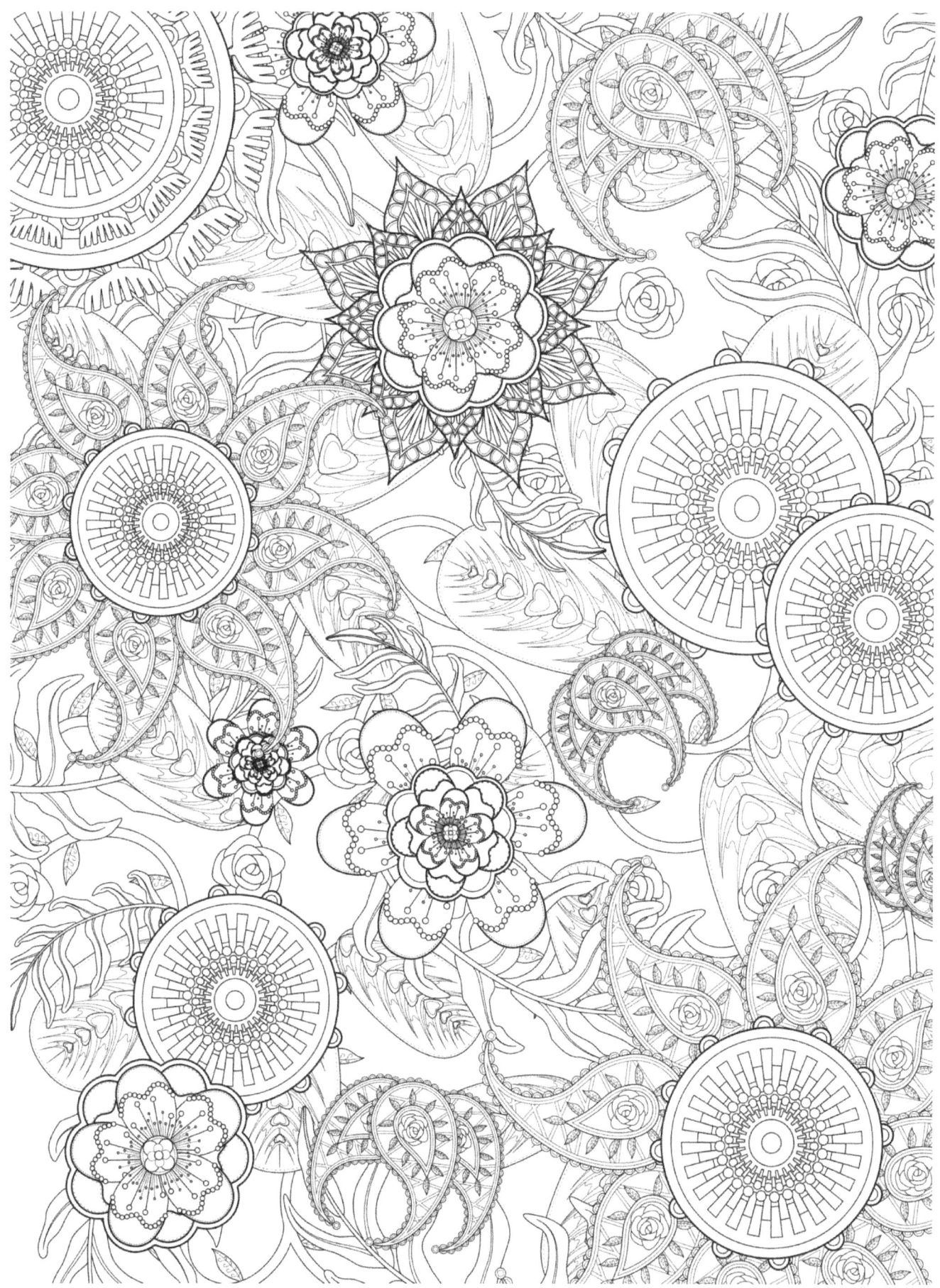

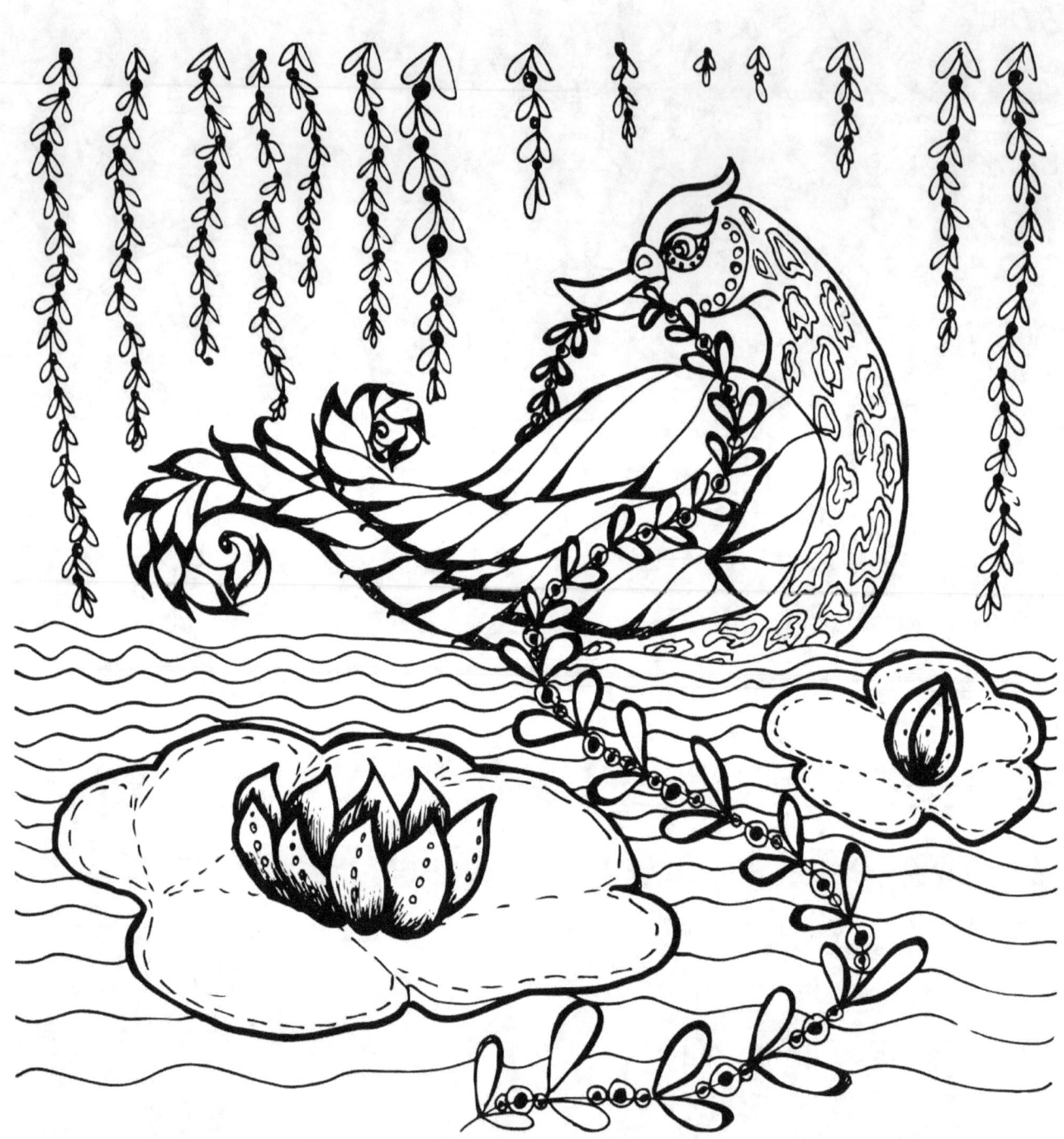

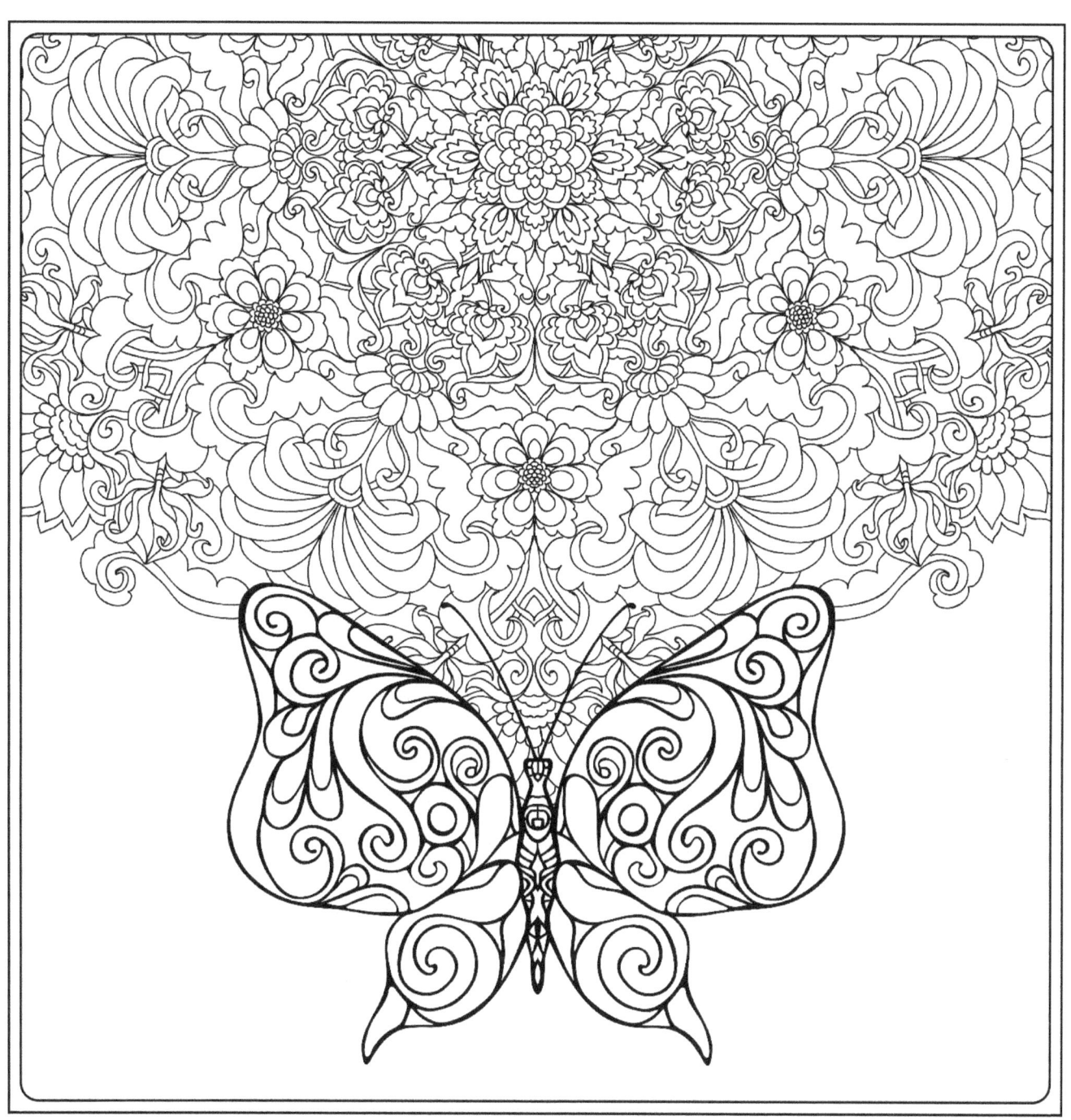

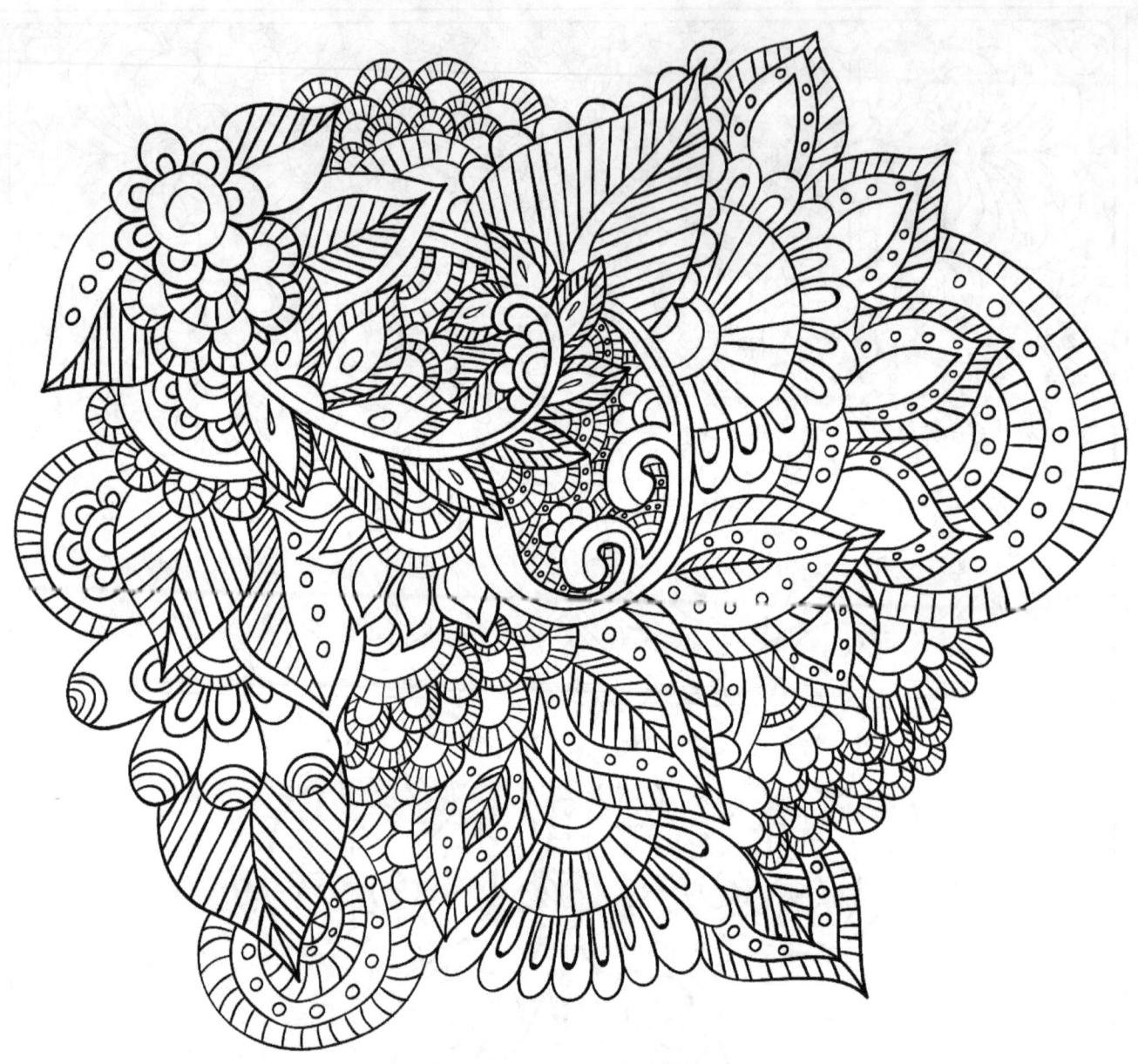

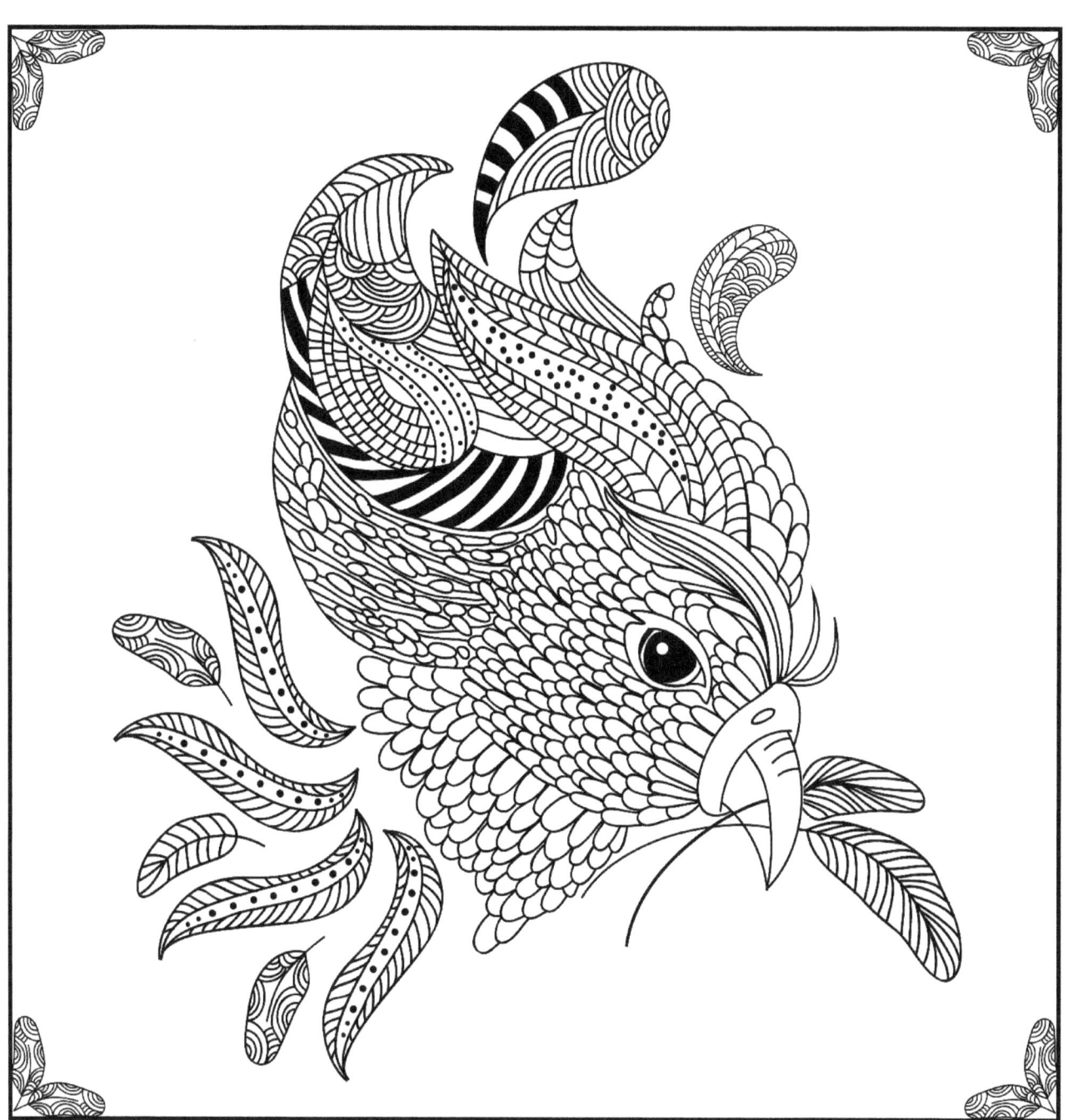

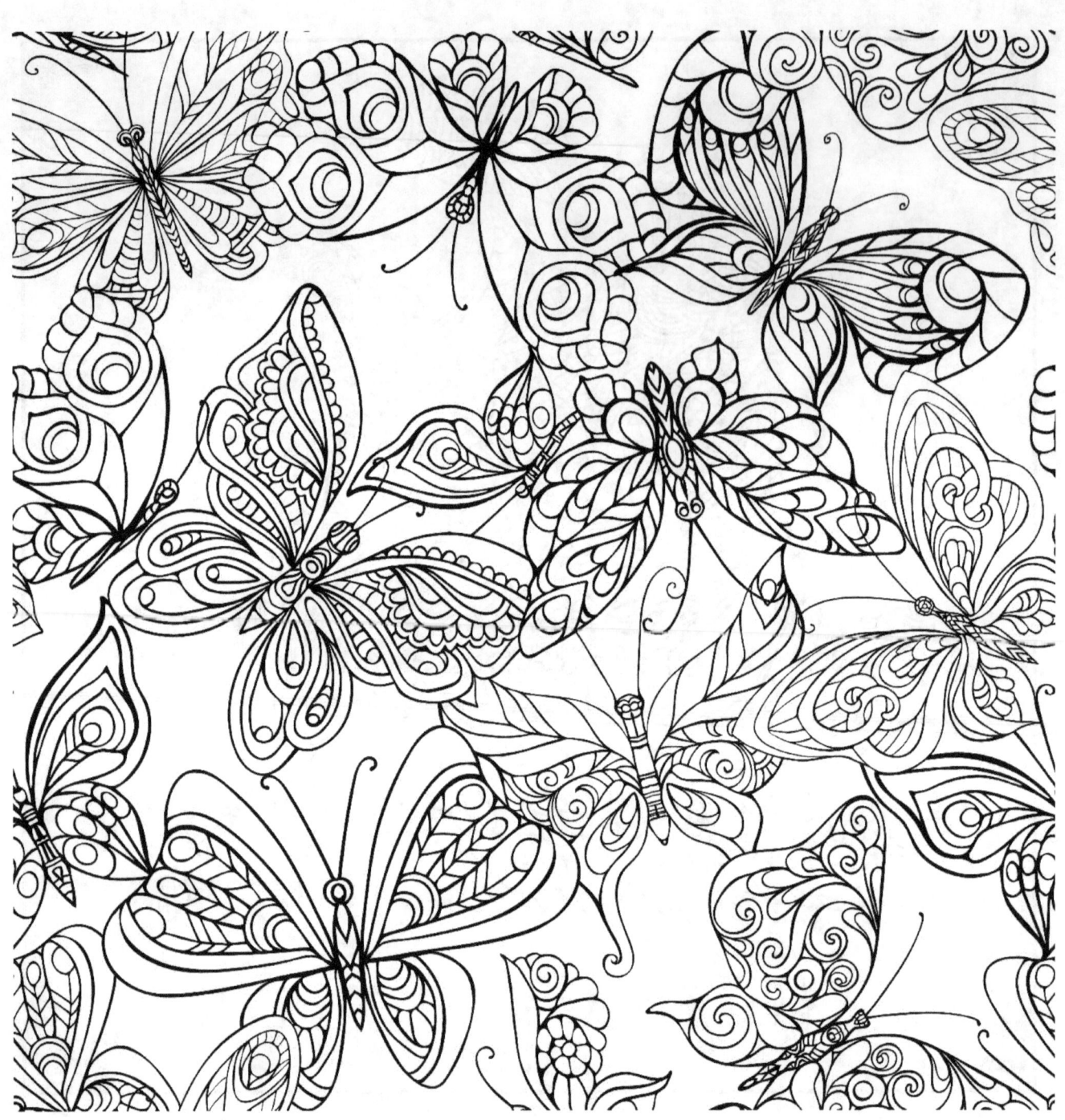

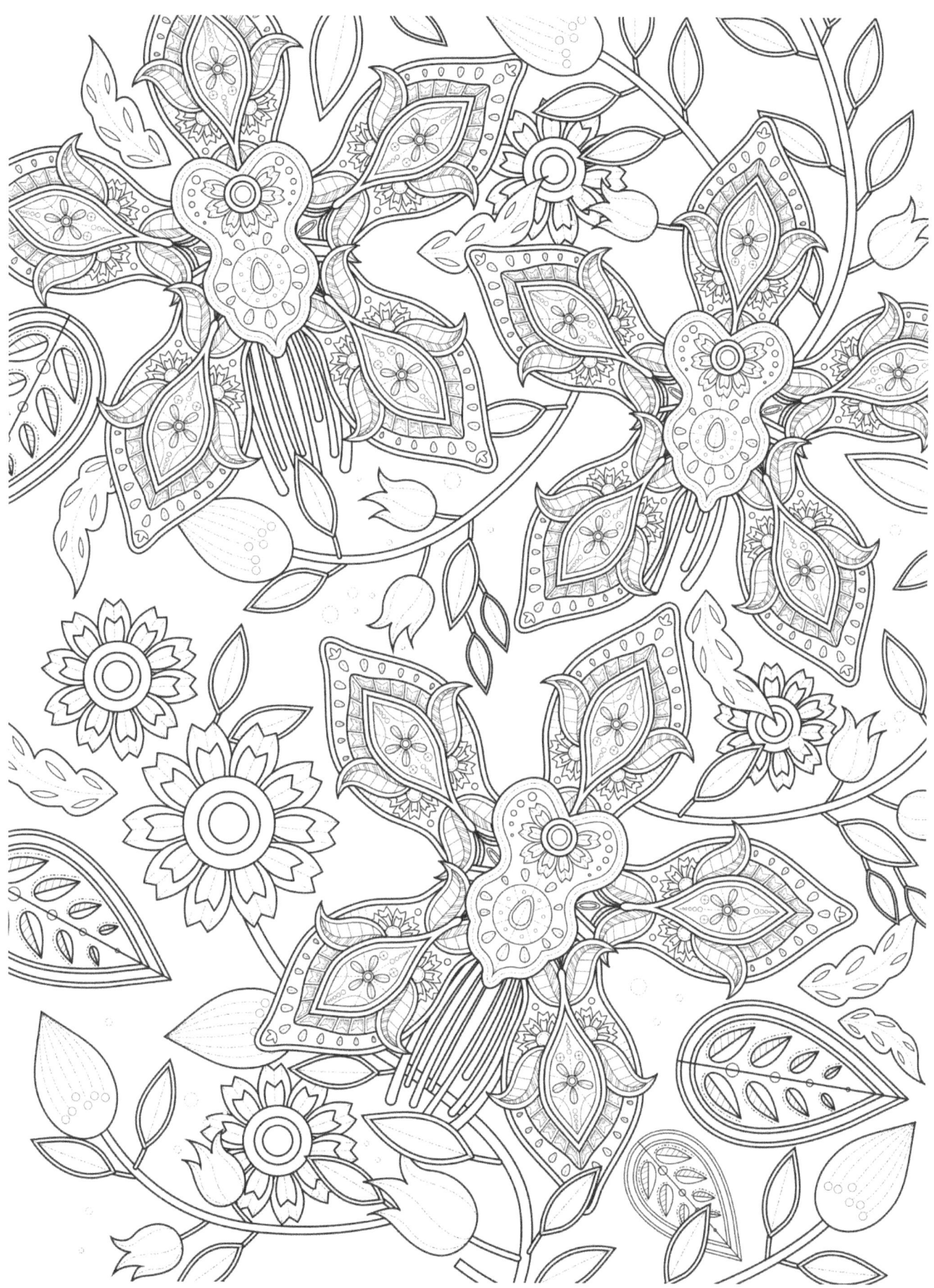

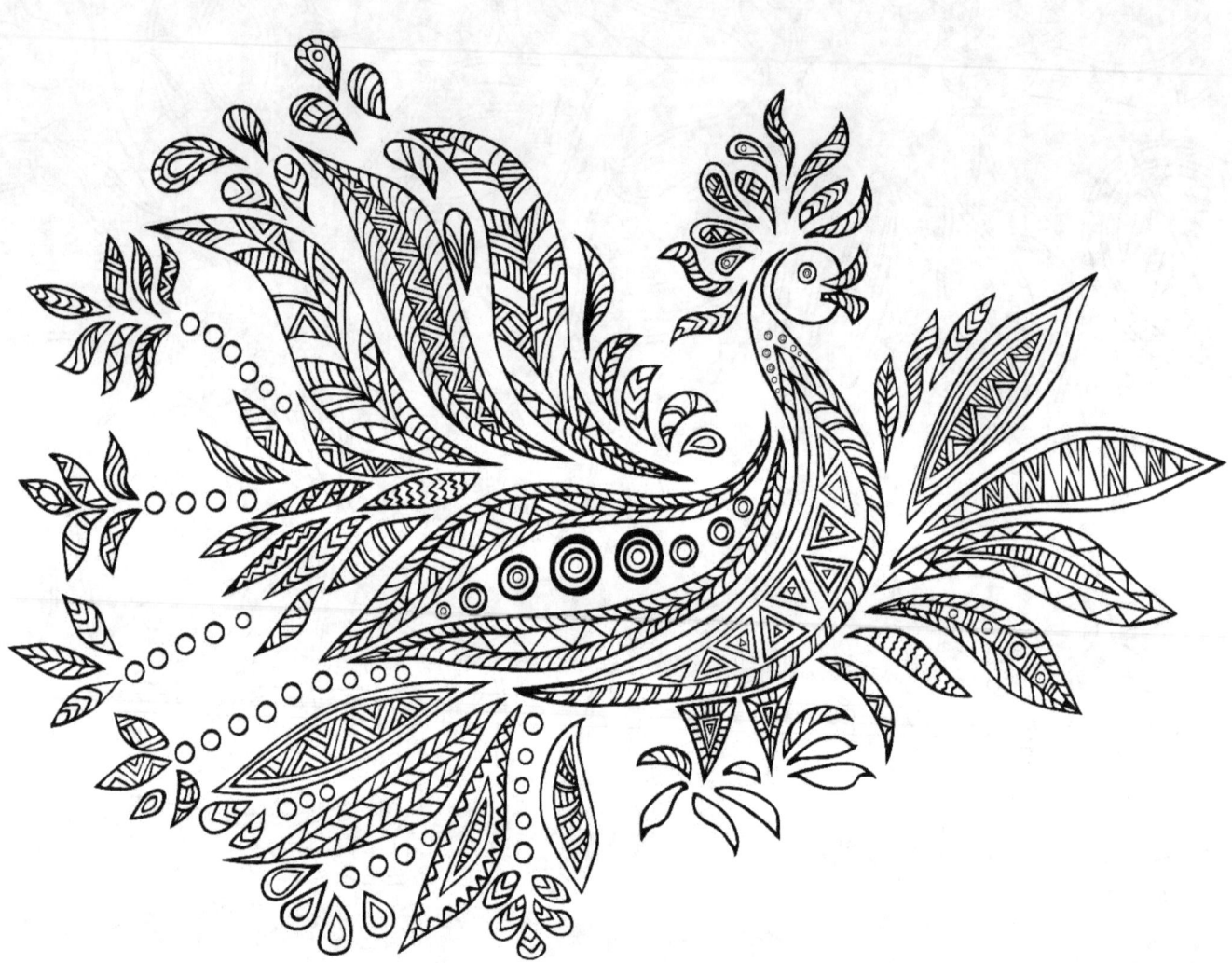

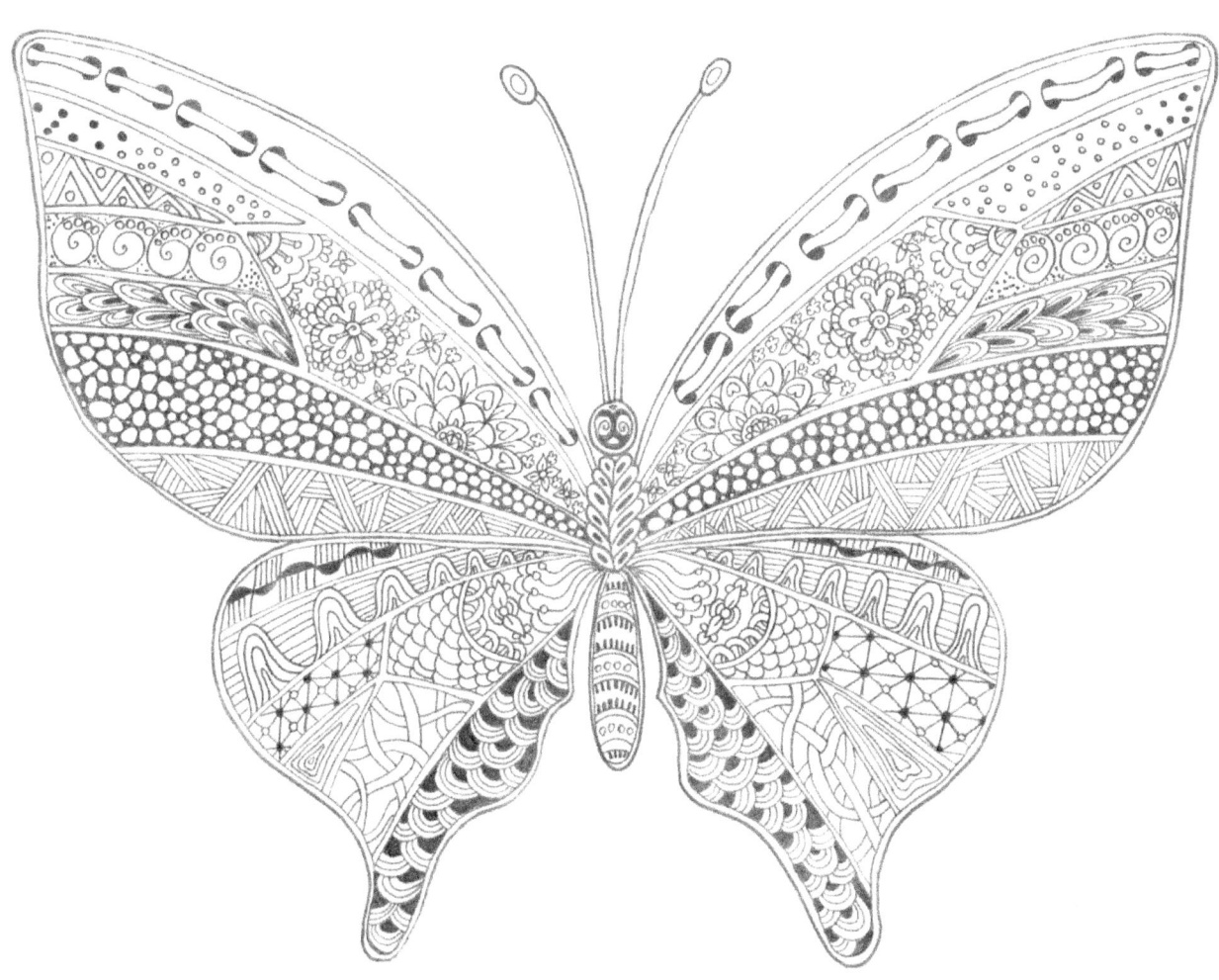

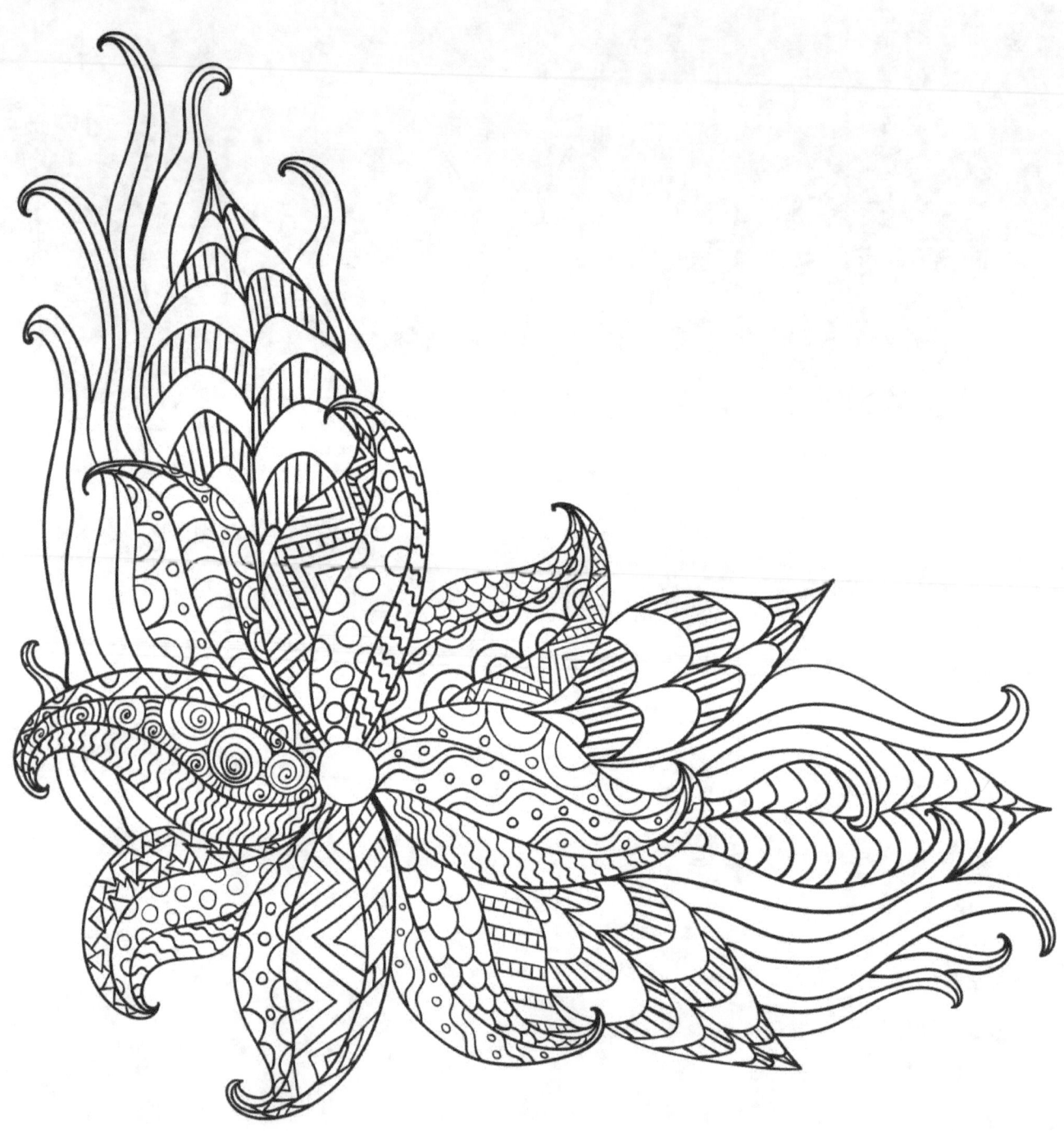

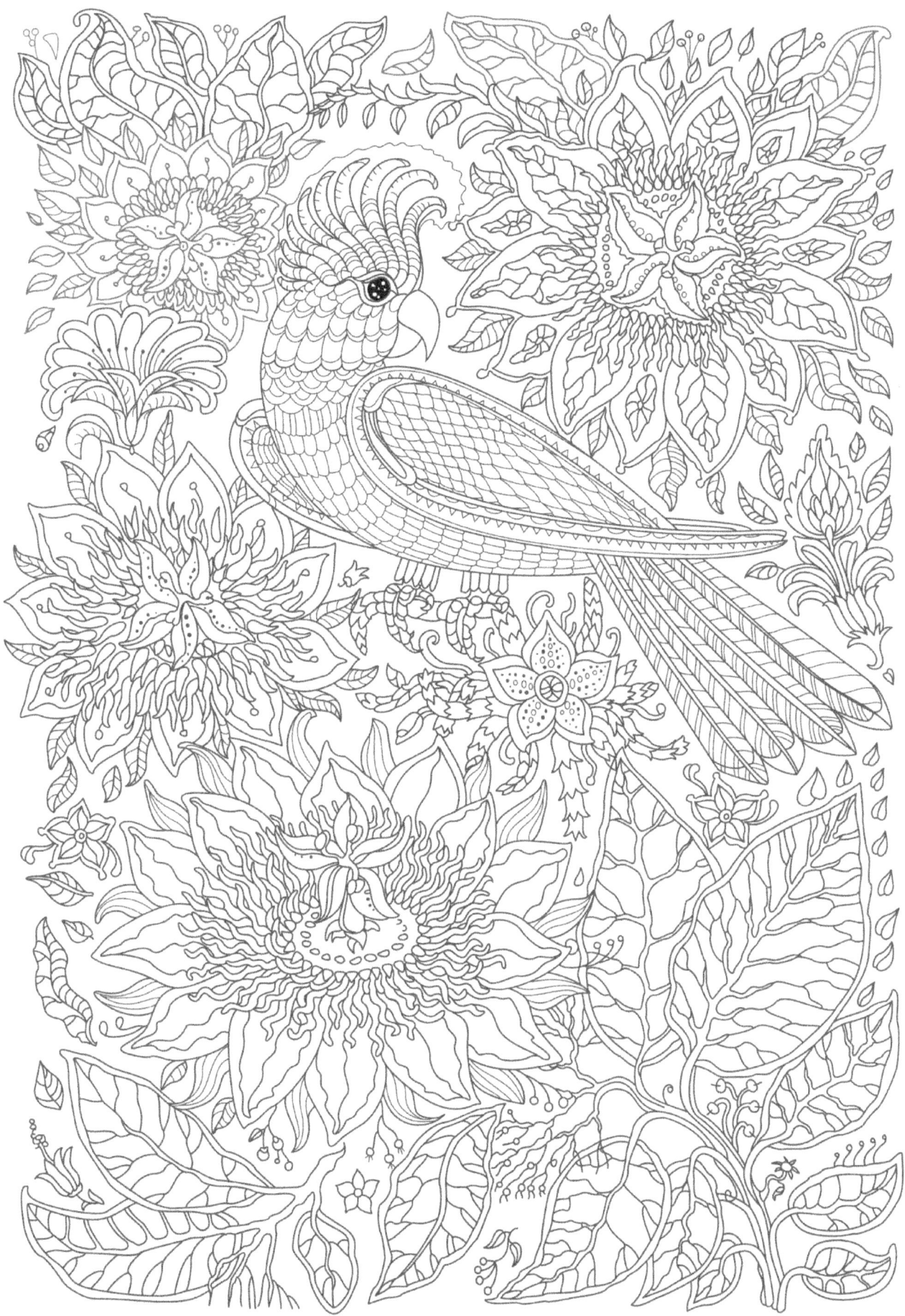

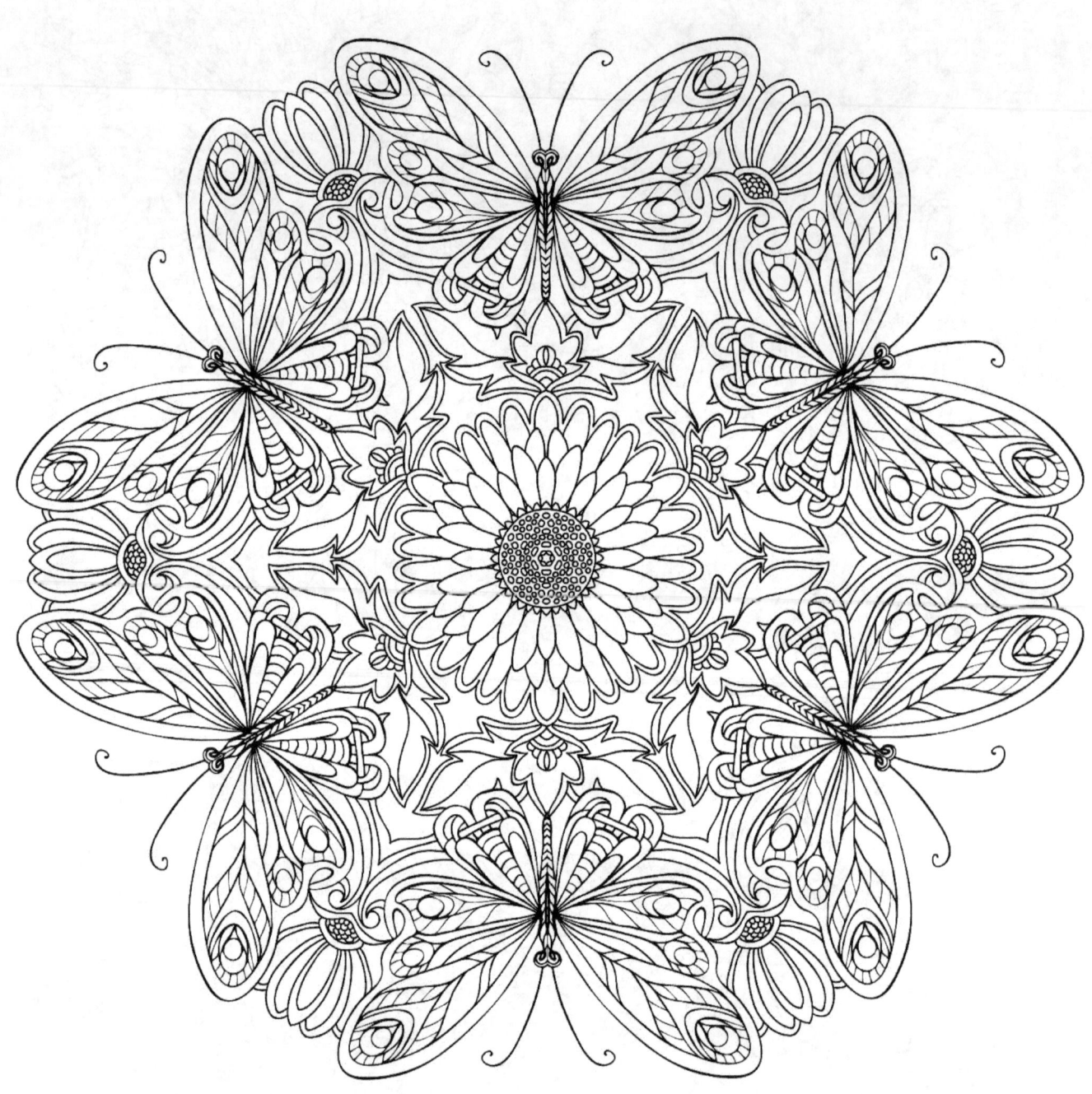

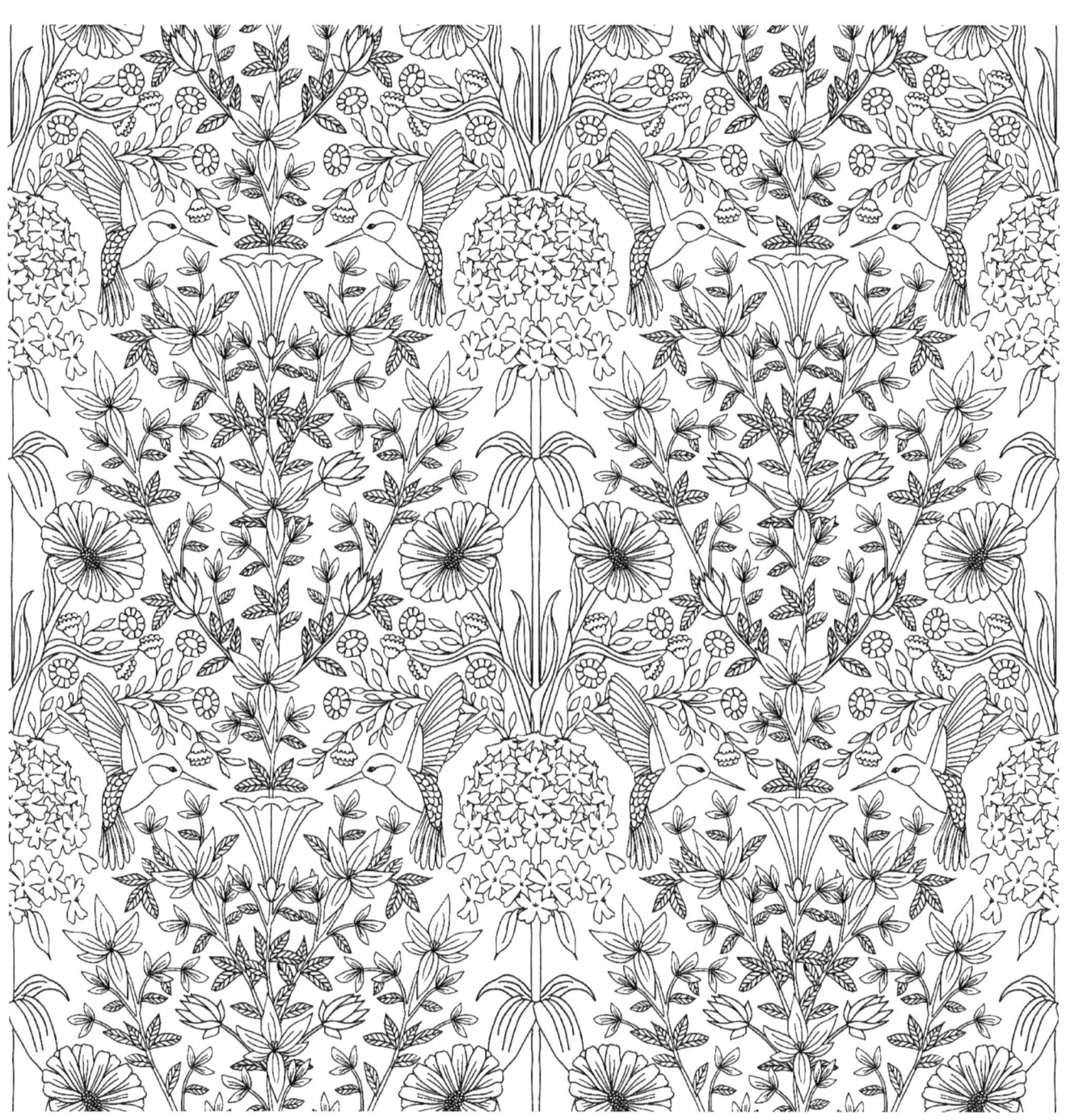

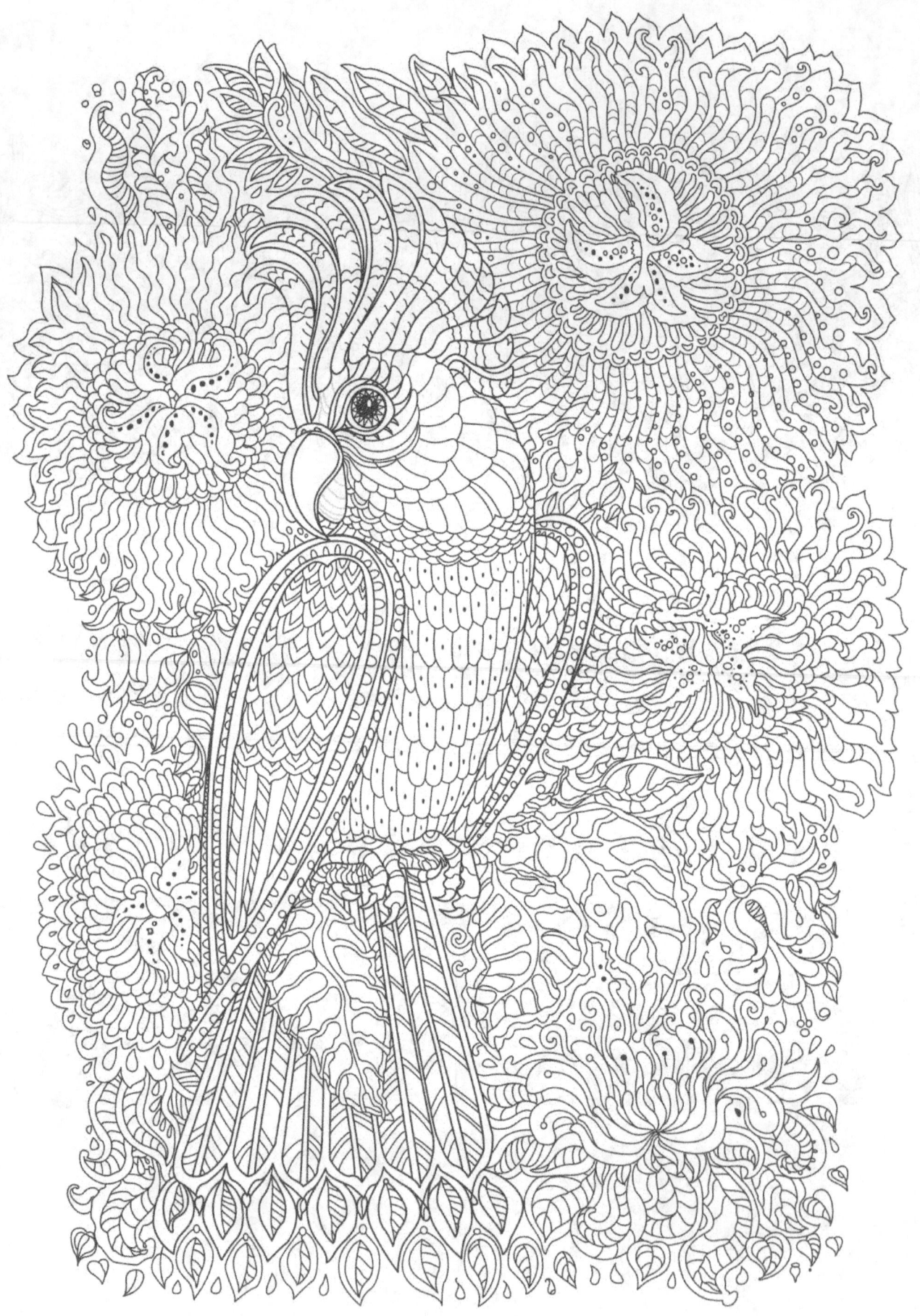

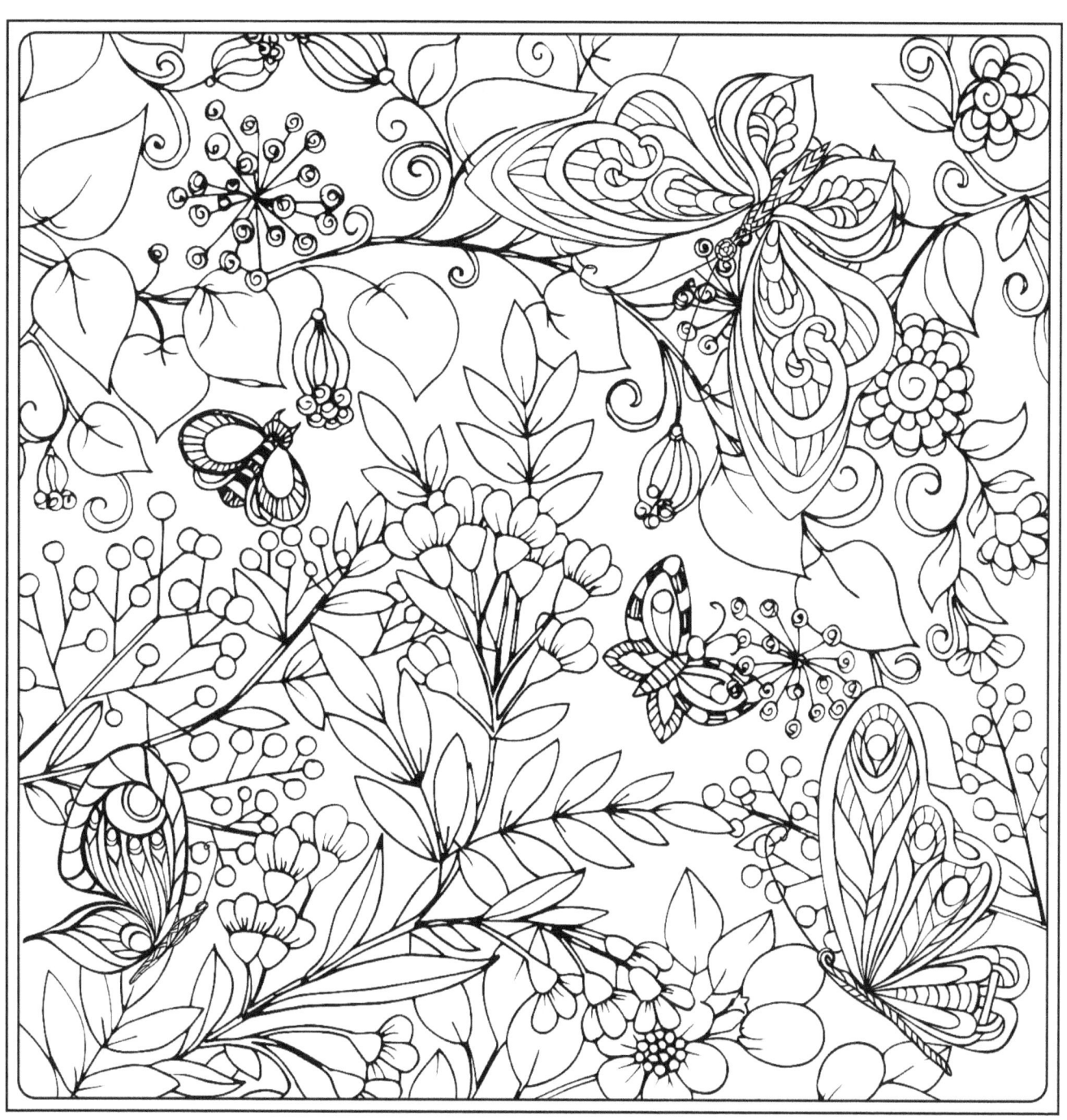

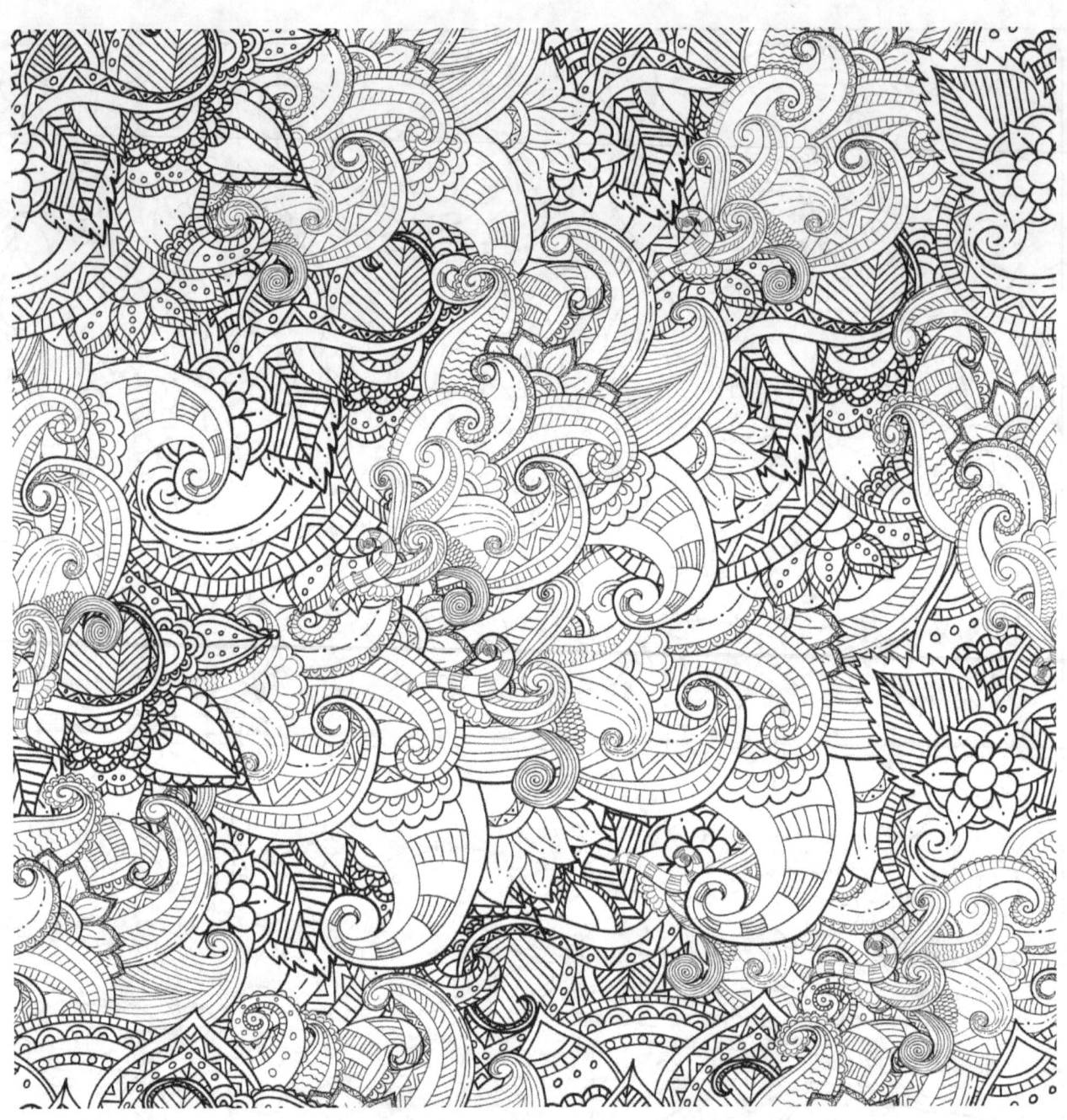

Kindle Users! Thank you for purchasing our book. We want to make it easy for you to get started coloring right away, so we are including a direct link to download this book:

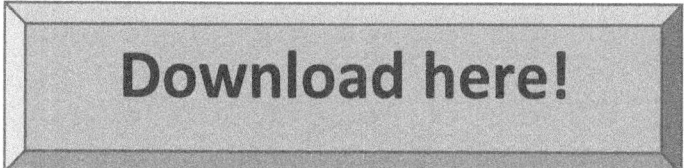

Or go to this page directly:

https://onedrive.live.com/redir?resid=4BBD7F9DAC2487E3!235&authkey=!AHejKTs1wopISGk&ithint=folder%2c